DI783739

# ACKNOWLEDGEMENTS

I would like to thank those who read drafts of part or all of this guide and made helpful comments: Balbir Chatrik (Youthaid), Duncan Lane (London Advice Services Alliance), Jackie McManus (Youthaid) and Paul Rennison (National Council for Vocational Qualifications).

I am also grateful to people working within the Department of Social Security, the Department for Education and Employment, the Employment Service, the Welsh Office and the Scottish Office for information, comments, corrections and answers to queries, and to people working in training schemes and advice centres for information given to Youthaid.

I gratefully acknowledge the financial support we have received from Bass PLC.

Finally, thanks to Nicola Bennett-Jones for her editing.

Youthaid remains responsible for the contents of this book.

# ABBREVIATIONS USED IN THIS GUIDE

| | |
|---|---|
| AO | Adjudication Officer |
| AOG | Adjudication Officers' Guide, 1996 |
| AIIS | Analogous Industrial Injuries Scheme |
| BA | Benefits Agency |
| CBEP | Child Benefit Extension Period |
| CCTE | Chambers of Commerce, Training and Enterprise |
| CPAG | Child Poverty Action Group |
| DLA | Disability Living Allowance |
| DfEE | Department for Education and Employment |
| DSS | Department of Social Security |
| ES | Employment Service |
| GNVQ | General National Vocational Qualification |
| IS | Income Support |
| ITP | Individual Training Plan |
| ITO | Industry Training Organisation |
| JSA | Jobseeker's Allowance |
| LEC | Local Enterprise Company (Scotland) |
| LMAO | Labour Market Adjudication Officer |
| NCVQ | National Council for Vocational Qualifications |
| NI | National Insurance |
| NRA | National Record of Achievement |
| NVQ | National Vocational Qualification |
| SAO | Sector Adjudication Officer |
| SDA | Severe Disablement Allowance |
| SHCU | Severe Hardship Claims Unit |
| SVQ | Scottish Vocational Qualification |
| TEC | Training and Enterprise Council (England and Wales) |
| TfW | Training for Work |
| YT | Youth Training |
| YTBA | Youth Training Bridging Allowance |
| YTS | Youth Training Scheme (before May 1990) |

Additional abbreviations are used for references to publications. These are listed under References (pages 145-7).

# CONTENTS

# ABOUT THIS GUIDE

In 1995/96 an average of 161,600 16 and 17 year olds were unemployed in Great Britain, not including those on training schemes. In 1996 on average 225,000 young people in England and Wales were on Youth Training and 41,000 on Modern Apprenticeships.

Most unemployed people under 18 are not entitled to benefits. Instead they are 'guaranteed' a place on Youth Training with a training allowance. However in 1995/96 on average 140,400 16 and 17 year olds were without an income: not in training, education or employment, or drawing benefits. For many the result is poverty and homelessness.

Young people, their parents and their advisers are often not aware of the rights young people have in training or to benefits. This Guide gives comprehensive information on these rights and on the procedures of the Government departments and other agencies responsible for young people's training and benefits. Part One of the Guide looks at the benefits available to 16 and 17 year olds. Part Two looks at Youth Credits, Youth Training, Modern Apprenticeships, National Traineeships and Relaunch.

## Sources

The Guide draws on a variety of sources. The Statutes or legal Regulations which underpin young people's rights have been identified where relevant. The legal information has been supplemented by drawing on the detailed guidance given to adjudication officers (AOs) on how they should decide issues about claimants' eligibility for benefit. It is important to emphasise that AOs are bound by the law contained in Regulations, but are **not bound to follow the guidance** outlined in their own, thirteen-volume, Adjudication Officers' Guide (AOG).

The primary sources of information about the rights of participants in Youth Training, Youth Credits and Modern Apprenticeships are legislation and the legal contracts made between Government departments and the many contractors who provide programmes. In particular we use the clauses contained in the *Training and Enterprise Council & Chambers of Commerce, Training and Enterprise (TEC & CCTE) Planning Prospectus* together with its associated documents: the *TEC & CCTE Finance Guide*, the *TEC & CCTE Management Information Guide*, the *TEC & CCTE Standards Guide*, the *TEC & CCTE Annual Funding Contract* and the *TEC & CCTE Licence*. These replace the old *TEC Operating Agreement* and the *Annual Funding Agreement*. Our references to the *Standards Guide* are to a draft as the final version was not available at the time of going to press. Paragraph numbers may differ in the final version.

Each TEC or CCTE has to abide by the requirements and meet the obligations spelt out in its *Licence* and *Annual Funding Contract,* which are part of its legal contract with the Government. In Scotland LECs contract with Scottish Enterprise or Highlands & Islands Enterprise. (An outline of the role of TECs and LECs is given on page 5.)

Detailed operating rules laid down by Scottish Enterprise/Highlands & Islands Enterprise for Scottish LECs are not available. Last year a Scottish Office minister stated that they closely followed the TEC contractual documents *(Hansard WA, 18/3/96, col 61)*.

The Welsh TEC Contract and Operating Manual broadly mirror the English documents but there are differences.

The Guide also draws on internal procedural guides and codes which have been issued to the staff of the Benefits Agency and the Employment Service.

Finally, where necessary we have supplemented these sources by written answers given by Government ministers to specific questions raised by Members of Parliament, both through correspondence and through the answers published in Hansard, the official record of parliamentary proceedings.

All these sources give a unique insight into the internal procedures and processes of the DSS, the Benefits Agency, the DfEE, the Employment Service and TECs/CCTEs/LECs and they can be invaluable when trying to secure fair treatment for young people. However, because the sources are not all based in law they do not necessarily imply that you have a legal right to be treated in a certain way. It is only where an Act of Parliament or a Regulation is referred to that you have a legal right.

Abbreviated references are used in the text. They are given in full at the end of the Guide.

## Changes in procedures and updating the Guide

It is important to note that many of the internal circulars, forms and procedures on which the Guide is based are changed from time to time. Clauses in the TEC/CCTE contractual documents can be revised during the course of the year. While the content of the Guide is accurate on going to press, it can be superseded by administrative or legal changes. We would encourage those interested in keeping up to date on these developments to subscribe to our regular monthly publication *Working Brief* (see page 150 for details).

If you find mistakes in the Guide, or if you obtain new information which ought to be included, please write to us so that we can rectify any errors and improve the content of future editions.

# Benefits and other guide books

For detailed information on the various training and employment schemes available to unemployed people aged over 18 and on the procedures to follow if you are not in full-time work and wish to claim benefit you should obtain *the Unemployment and Training Rights Handbook*, which is produced by the Unemployment Unit (see page 149 for details).

Child Poverty Action Group (CPAG) produces two annual publications which give comprehensive guidance on benefits and benefit entitlement – the *National Welfare Benefits Handbook* and the *Rights Guide to Non-Means-Tested Benefits*. They are available from CPAG Ltd, 1–5 Bath Street, London EC1V 9PY. You may be able to consult a copy of these at your local library or a local resource centre.

*A Guide to Housing Benefit and Council Tax Benefit* is available from Shelter at 88 Old Street, London EC1V 9HU. The Housing Campaign for Single Homeless People (CHAR) produces *The Benefits Guide: the comprehensive and easy to use guide to means tested benefits*, available from 5–15 Cromer Street, London WC1H 8LS. The annual *Disability Rights Handbook* can be obtained from the Disability Alliance, Universal House, 88–94 Wentworth Street, London E1 7SA.

# Further advice

If you experience difficulty with benefits or your rights on a scheme, and you need more specific advice, contact your nearest Legal Advice Centre, Welfare Rights Unit, Citizens Advice Bureau or Unemployed Workers Centre – addresses can be found in the phone book or your local library. These organisations can give free advice and, if you wish to appeal against a decision, will sometimes go to a tribunal with you. More specific advice may be available from your trade union, if you are a member, or from a student welfare officer or student union at your college.

# *INTRODUCTION*
# DEPARTMENTS AND AGENCIES.

Two government departments have the main responsibility for training programmes and benefits for young people – the Department for Education and Employment (DfEE) and the Department of Social Security (DSS). The Department of Social Security is now in the process of handing over responsibility for Jobseeker's Allowance (JSA) for young people to the Employment Service.

## The Department of Social Security and the Benefits Agency

The DSS is responsible for Income Support and Child Benefit. Since April 1991 most of its services have been delivered through the Benefits Agency (BA) which operates a national network of local offices. You can get the address and telephone number of your local Benefits Agency office from your local library or telephone directory.

## The Department for Education and Employment

In the 1980s most employment and training services were delivered either directly by the Employment Department or through the related Manpower Services Commission. During the 1990s most of these activities have been transferred to new types of organisation which operate through commercial performance-related annual contracts – the Employment Service (ES), Training and Enterprise Councils (TECs), Scottish Enterprise, Highlands & Islands Enterprise and Local

Enterprise Companies (LECs). In 1992 the Welsh Office took over responsibility for training and enterprise activities within Wales. The Employment Department merged with the Department for Education in 1995 to become the Department for Education and Employment.

# The Employment Service

The Employment Service (ES) became an Executive Agency in April 1990. It operates through a contract with the DfEE, of which it remains a part. The ES runs Jobcentres.

Jobcentres are responsible for paying JSA. Both ES and BA staff placed within the Jobcentre are involved. The ES is directly responsible for paying Bridging Allowance (see page 19).

The aim is that by April 1998, ES and BA services to young people claiming JSA will everywhere be delivered by the same person. Where this is not yet possible, claims are dealt with by an **ES Adviser** for the labour market aspects and a **BA 16/17 Year Olds Claim Specialist** for the payment aspects.

Within Jobcentres, the **ES Business Manager** is responsible for ensuring that *(JSA 16/17 Ch 1 para 6)*:
+ systems and resources can deal with emergency cases;
+ ES and BA officers work smoothly as a team to provide a 'seamless' service;
+ claims from young people are dealt with within 48 hours and sooner if at all possible;
+ adequate private interviewing facilities are provided;

and for:
+ liaison arrangements with all relevant parties;
+ working relationships with the Careers Service;
+ referral forms, Jobseeker's Agreements, decisions by advisers acting on behalf of the Secretary of State, referrals to the Guarantee Liaison Officer, and good cause certificates.

The **Nominated BA HEO** is responsible for *(JSA 16/17 Ch 1 para 7)*:

✦ payment;

✦ liaising with the ES Business Manager and others;

✦ liaising with outside agencies and groups;

✦ recommendations to the Severe Hardship Claims Unit to issue Certificates of Authority (for BA officers to decide claims under Severe Hardship provision);

✦ deciding if a referral to the police and/or Social Services should be made without a young person's consent where there is evidence of serious physical or sexual abuse;

✦ ensuring that all officers who deal with young people on payment issues and those making severe hardship decisions have had the right training.

Each is responsible for ensuring that enough officers are trained to provide adequate cover and deal with claims.

During 1997 responsibility for services to young people will shift to the ES.

## Good practice

The BA/ES guidance volume *JSA for 16 and 17 year olds* warns that a young person may be distressed or confused by the process of making a claim; if so the ES adviser should take time to explain matters carefully.

You can take someone into the interview with you. There have been cases when advocates have, wrongly, been told that they cannot go in with a young person or, if they do, that they cannot speak.

## Appeals

If you do not agree with the decision about your benefits you may be able to appeal to an independent social security appeal tribunal. A tribunal can look at appeals against any decision taken by an adjudication officer about your IS/JSA (for example, if you are being paid the lower rate and think you should get the higher rate), but not about whether you qualify for payments under severe hardship provision (see below).

To help you in your appeal you should ask the Jobcentre for a written statement of the reasons for the decision. The appeal must be made in writing within three months of the written decision being sent to you. A late appeal can be accepted for 'special reasons' that are 'wholly exceptional'. For more details see the CPAG's *National Welfare Benefits Handbook*, Chapter 8 (see page xviii). It would be useful to get representation: (see 'Further Advice' on page xviii).

You cannot appeal against decisions made by the Secretary of State, such as whether you will get JSA under the severe hardship provision. You can write to the Severe Hardship Claims Unit (see page 37) and/or to the manager of your local Jobcentre if you believe that certain facts have not been taken into consideration or if your circumstances changed. You can also contact your MP. The only course of legal action you can take is to apply to the High Court for judicial review.

As part of the Citizen's Charter initiative the ES introduced its own Jobseeker's Charter in January 1992. This sets out the help and minimum standards of service that should be available. A leaflet explaining the nature of the Jobseeker's Charter should be available in Jobcentres.

Another leaflet, *Help Us To Get It Right and How To Complain*, sets out a complaints and suggestions procedure; an accompanying envelope is addressed to the local Jobcentre manager.

A written complaint should be 'responded to within five working days or an acknowledgement sent'. An acknowledgement should explain 'who is dealing with the complaint and when they are likely to reply'. If the manager feels the complaint would be better dealt with face to face s/he may suggest an interview.

If you do not feel that your complaint has been satisfactorily answered you can contact your MP. If your MP does not get a satisfactory response s/he may take up your case with the Parliamentary Ombudsman.

## The Parliamentary Ombudsman

Executive Agencies, such as the ES and the Benefits Agency, are subject to scrutiny by the Parliamentary Commissioner for Administration – the Parliamentary Ombudsman. The Ombudsman is independent of Government and can investigate complaints of maladministration made by members of the public that are taken up by Members of Parliament.

Examples of maladministration include unreasonable delay, failure to make timely payments, rudeness and the loss of papers. Complaints should show that some injustice has been caused and should be made within a year. If after investigation the Ombudsman finds the complaint is justified, s/he can propose appropriate redress, such as an apology and/or compensation.

## TECs and LECs

A comprehensive national network of 82 TECs in England and Wales and 22 LECs in Scotland was established in 1991. With the demise of South Thames TEC, the merger of Centec and Cilntec, and the merger of North East Wales and Targed, there are now 79 organisations in England and Wales. Some TECs have merged with their local Chamber of Commerce to become a Chamber of Commerce, Training and Enterprise (CCTE). In this book we refer to TECs when we mean Training and Enterprise Councils and/or Chambers of Commerce, Training and Enterprise. (A list of the names and addresses of TECs and LECs appears in Appendix B.)

These organisations are responsible for delivering most training schemes. In 1996/97 TECs in England controlled some £1.5 billion of public funds from the DfEE in addition to money from other sources. TECs in Wales controlled about £117 million and LECs in Scotland controlled about £461 million.

At least two-thirds of the directors of each TEC and LEC, including the chairperson, must be chairpersons or senior executives from the private sector. The remaining directors are senior figures in the local community who support the aims of the TEC. The directors are on the board as individuals, not as representatives of their organisations *(TEC Standards (draft), para C3)*.

Each TEC is an independent company which enters into a contract with the Secretaries of State for Education and Employment, the Environment, and Trade and Industry or with the Secretary of State for Wales. In Scotland the LECs enter into contracts with either Scottish Enterprise or Highlands & Islands Enterprise, which have substantial powers under the 1990 Enterprise and New Towns (Scotland) Act.

TECs and LECs are responsible for delivering Youth Training (YT), Youth Credits (Skillseekers in Scotland), Modern Apprenticeships and National Traineeships. They are also involved in delivering guidance, enterprise and education programmes and other training programmes such as Training for Work (for more details on these see the *Unemployment and Training Rights Handbook* listed on page 149). In Scotland LECs play a part in delivering the economic development activities formerly carried out by the Scottish Development Agency and the Highlands & Islands Development Board.

TECs and LECs can provide some services directly, but mainly they sub-contract their programmes to other providers. They are responsible for ensuring that these providers deliver good quality training and meet the terms and conditions outlined in their contracts with the Government (or in Scotland with Scottish Enterprise/Highlands &

Islands Enterprise). One of their first priorities is to ensure that there are enough YT places available to meet the YT Guarantees.

TECs and LECs have been given certain contractual 'flexibilities' to design schemes to meet local needs and achieve better value for money. As individual TEC and LEC policies influence local provision, there is an increasing diversity in the programmes they run. However, though the names of local programmes may vary, as may the terms and conditions of trainees, the programmes are still subject to the national rules outlined in the relevant chapters.

The way in which the TECs and LECs run their programmes is also influenced by the funding system. In 1997/98, the DfEE and the Welsh Office will pay TECs on the basis of starts in training (around 20%), numbers in training (around 50%) and the achievement of agreed outputs (around 30%). The output-related funding is mainly related to young people achieving NVQ level 2 (or equivalent) or above, including Modern Apprenticeships leading to NVQ level 3. TECs can also claim output payments within YT for trainees endorsed as having a special training need who achieve qualifications at and below NVQ level 1.

In Scotland YT funding is allocated on the basis of the numbers starting on the programme (15%), the achievement of milestones (45%) and the achievement of approved qualifications.

TECs do not have to replicate the way the DfEE funds them in the arrangements they negotiate with their suppliers, though they are expected to pass on the benefits of changes. In some areas certain schemes, for instance those working with people with special training needs, are given a lower percentage of output-related funding. However there has generally been pressure on TECs/LECs and training providers to favour young people who are expected to be high achievers.

## TEC and LEC accountability

TECs and LECs have to make certain information public, and have to announce and hold a public meeting at least once a year *(TEC Standards (draft), para C8.3)*. These requirements give other organisations an opportunity to influence local policy and to obtain information about how local flexibilities have been used.

A TEC has to allow public access to a summary of its Corporate Plan at its registered office *(TEC Standards (draft), para C8.1)*. It must publish at least a summary of its Business Plan within three months of the Business Plan being agreed *(TEC Standards (draft), para C8.2)*.

In addition a TEC must produce and publish an Annual Report and audited statement of accounts within nine months of the end of each contract year *(TEC Standards (draft), para C8.4)*. In Wales it must be produced within four months of the financial year.

The Annual Report must include a statement of the TEC's equal opportunities targets and details of its performance in relation to them *(TEC Standards (draft), para C4.1)*.

LECs in Scotland are subject to similar requirements.

## TECs and prohibited activities

TECs must not, except with the prior written agreement of the Secretary of State for Education and Employment, use their funds or assets or allow any of their subcontractors to use any TEC funds to 'support any organisation or activity which is likely to bring any of the Secretaries of State or the TEC/CCTE into disrepute'. They also must not enter into or allow their subcontractors to enter into 'any agreement involving the use of TEC/CCTE funds with any political or religious organisation if the effect of that agreement would be to promote a particular political or religious view' *(TEC Standards (draft), para A3.4, A3.5)*.

## TECs and quality assurance

TECs must be able to demonstrate that they have appropriate internal Quality Assurance systems *(TEC Standards (draft), para B5.2)*. They must also demonstrate that they have and are implementing strategies for Quality Assurance of their suppliers *(TEC Standards (draft), para C6)*.

The standard arrangements 'require TECs to operate comprehensive and disciplined systems in the way they contract for and manage all services and products which the Department funds' *(TEC QA, 1993, p2)*. TECs are required to implement detailed arrangements which ensure, among other things, that *(TEC QA, 1993, p3-4)*:

✦ clear and measurable outputs and standards are specified for each of the services and products it requires;

✦ TECs and their suppliers have the resources and the skills to meet the obligations before contracting;

✦ suppliers clearly identify the individuals responsible for the delivery of each service and product;

✦ the TEC and supplier agree and document a comprehensive progress review process; and

✦ suppliers systematically evaluate their delivery of products and services.

TEC suppliers will be required to operate a system for 'collecting customer feedback on the services and products which they deliver and on the processes through which they have been delivered'. This 'feedback will lead to appropriate action to deal with criticisms or suggestions'.

## PART ONE
# BENEFITS FOR UNEMPLOYED
# 16 AND 17 YEAR OLDS

### Under 18 and unemployed

If you are under 18 and unemployed, there are limited circumstances in which you can get benefit. However, you have a right to make a claim and should not be turned away by your local Jobcentre. If you are not in work or full-time education you are guaranteed a Youth Training (YT) place (see Part Two of this Guide). If you are not entitled to benefit this may be your only way to get an income.

You or your parents may get short-term payments while you are looking for a suitable YT place in the form of 'extended' **Child Benefit** or **YT Bridging Allowance**. The rules for claiming both of these are explained in this part of the Guide.

The 1988 Social Security Act raised the normal minimum age for claiming **Income Support** (IS) from 16 to 18 years, but some people aged 16 and 17 can still receive IS or **Jobseeker's Allowance** (JSA) in certain circumstances. The Secretary of State for Social Security also has powers to make discretionary JSA payments in cases of 'severe hardship'. All young people with little or no money who make a claim for JSA and do not fall into the 'prescribed groups' (see page 28) should be considered for JSA under the severe hardship provision.

These exceptions to the general withdrawal of benefit are supposed to provide a safety net for young people. However on 13 March 1989 Nicholas Scott, the Minister for Social Security, acknowledged that the withdrawal of IS from most young people had left some 'facing real difficulties'.

Youthaid estimates that during 1995/96 an average of 140,400 young people in Great Britain were without a job, a YT place or any benefit. The system of payments for 16 and 17 year olds is so complex that many young people, and some local Benefits Agency offices and Jobcentres, are unclear about entitlements. The rules for IS and JSA entitlement are explained in this part of the Guide.

## Under 16 and unemployed

Entitlement to IS *(SSC&B Act 1992, section 124)* and JSA *(JS Act 1995, section 3(1)(f))* cannot begin before 16. You are not allowed to claim until you are 16 even if you are 15 when you legitimately leave school. If you live with your parents or other adults they can claim Child Benefit and any relevant benefit dependency addition. If you live away from your parents or guardian you are expected to get help from social services.

# CHILD BENEFIT

## While in 'relevant education'

While you are under 19 and in 'relevant' education your parents can claim Child Benefit for you. If your parents are entitled to claim IS/JSA themselves, they can also claim for you (see page 18). If you do not live with your parents or guardian and therefore no one is claiming Child Benefit for you, you may be able to claim IS in your own right (see page 30).

> **'Relevant' education** is 'non-advanced' (up to and including A levels or higher level Scottish certificate of education) and lasts more than 12 hours a week not counting homework or other unsupervised study and meal breaks *(IS (Gen) Regs, reg 12; CB (Gen) Regs, reg 1(2), reg 5(2), reg 7A)*.

You are considered as being in relevant education until the end of the holiday after the term in which you leave. This day is called the **terminal date**. Child Benefit is always paid on a Monday for the period up to the following Sunday. When you leave relevant education, it should be paid up to and including the Sunday following the terminal date, unless you find a job or YT place before then *(AOG, vol 9, para 55302)*.

If you leave school before the legal school leaving date, you will be treated as having stayed on until that date *(AOG, vol 6, para 35534)*. If you leave after the legal school leaving date, for Child Benefit purposes you will be treated as if you stayed on until the end of the term in which you actually leave. If you are registered for any external exams, you count as leaving school after the date of the exam(s) even if you do not go to school during that term and you do not take the exam(s) *(CB (Gen) Regs, reg 7(5)&(6))*.

This means that, in England and Wales, unless you become 18 or start work or YT, when you leave full-time education Child Benefit can continue until whichever of the following Mondays comes first *(AOG, vol 9, para 55303)*:
◆ the first Monday in January;
◆ the Monday following Easter Monday;
◆ the first Monday in September.

The Child Benefit paid on this date will cover the period up to the following Sunday. If you become 18 or start work or YT before this date, Child Benefit stops from the Monday following the day on which you start work or YT, or the Monday of or following your 18th birthday.

In Scotland the same basic rules apply. However, because of the different school leaving dates, Child Benefit may be paid for longer depending on when your 16th birthday falls. For example, if you leave school on the last day of the Winter term, but your 16th birthday is in the following January or February, Child Benefit will be paid until the Monday of or following your 16th birthday.

## The date you can legally leave school

**England and Wales** *(Education (School Leaving Dates) Act 1976)*:
◆ the last day of the Spring term if you reach 16 between
1 September and 31 January inclusive;
◆ the Friday before the last Monday in May if you reach 16 between
1 February and 31 August inclusive.

**Scotland** *(Education (Scotland) Act 1980)*:
◆ 31 May if you reach 16 between 1 March and 30 September
inclusive;
◆ the first day of the Christmas holiday period if you reach 16
between 1 October and the last day of February inclusive.

# Child Benefit Extension Period

If you are 16 or 17 and live with your parent(s) or guardian they can claim Child Benefit for an extended period after you leave school. The Child Benefit Extension Period (CBEP) starts on the Monday after the terminal date (see above) *(CB (Gen) Regs, reg 7D (2)(a))*. During this period you are expected to find a job or YT place. If you don't live with your parent(s) or guardian you may be able to claim JSA during this period (see page 34).

| Time of leaving school | The CBEP |
|---|---|
| In the term up to Christmas | 12 weeks from and including the second Monday in January |
| In the term up to Easter | 12 weeks from and including the second Monday after Easter Monday |
| In the term up to the Summer holidays | From the second Monday in September up to and including the Sunday before the first Monday in January. This can be either 16 or 17 weeks depending on the year. |

*(CB (Gen) Regs, reg 7D(2)(b))*

## CBEP dates 1997

| Term of leaving school | Terminal date | | Start of CBEP | End of CBEP |
|---|---|---|---|---|
| Winter 1996 | 1st Monday in January: | 6/1/97 | 13/1/97 | 6/4/97 |
| Spring 1997 | 1st Monday after Easter Monday: | 7/4/97 | 14/4/97 | 6/7/97 |
| Summer 1997 | 1st Monday in September: | 1/9/97 | 8/9/97 | 4/1/98 |
| Winter 1997 | 1st Monday in January: | 5/1/98 | 12/1/98 | 5/4/98 |

## How to claim extended Child Benefit

The Child Benefit Branch of the DSS should automatically send your parents a letter (form CH(A)298) asking about your future plans before the date you legally leave school. If this does not happen, for example if you leave school earlier than intended, your parents can ask about entitlement at your local Benefits Agency office or by writing to the Child Benefit Centre (Washington), PO Box 1, Newcastle upon Tyne, NE88 1AA.

If your parents want to continue to claim Child Benefit during the extension period they should fill in Part C on page 4 of the form CH(A)298 and send it back in the envelope provided.

| When you are legally allowed to leave school | When the Child Benefit Branch should send your parents the form CH(A)298 |
| --- | --- |
| Summer term | Mid-July |
| End of Christmas term | Mid-November |
| End of Easter term | Usually in February (but this depends on the date of Easter) |

Extended Child Benefit can be claimed if:

✦ you have not already started work or YT and you are registered for work or a YT place at a Careers Service office. (Registration may have taken place at your school. If you are unsure of the date, the Careers Service can help.)

✦ you are planning to go on to advanced education – you must still register at a Careers Service office.

**Child Benefit should not be withdrawn if you refuse a job or a YT place during the CBEP.**

Extended Child Benefit will end when one of the following happens, whichever comes first:

◆ you receive IS/JSA yourself *(CB (Gen) Regs 7C & 7D(3)(b))*;

◆ you start a job (of at least 24 hours a week) or YT course;

◆ you start a course of advanced education;

◆ you reach your 18th birthday (your last Child Benefit will be paid on the Monday before this date – you may then be able to claim JSA);

◆ the end of the CBEP.

On the form CH(A)298 your parent/guardian has to give the date on which you registered with the Careers Service and has to sign the following declaration:

> "I will let you know straight away if s/he starts paid work or a YT course, receives Income Support or Jobseeker's Allowance in her/his own right or starts a course of advanced education."

If you leave school before you are 18, but after the date you can legally leave school, extended Child Benefit can be paid from the end of the holiday after the term in which you left.

## Reclaiming extended Child Benefit

Child Benefit will stop if you find work or go into YT. It can be paid again if you leave YT or a job within the CBEP, whatever the reason for leaving. You will need to register for a job or YT place at a Careers Service office. Your parents should then reclaim Child Benefit, normally on a form CH298(LO). This form is available from your local Benefits Agency office or from the Child Benefit Centre (address above).

If you lose your job or YT place because of sickness during the CBEP your parents can reclaim Child Benefit using the form CH298(LO). Again you must register for work or a YT place at the Careers Service office. If you are too sick to go to the office your parents can contact the local Careers Service office either in person or by phone to confirm your intention of finding a YT place once you are well again.

## Child Benefit and other benefits

*IS/JSA*

If your parents receive IS/JSA they will get a personal allowance and any relevant premiums for you if they receive Child Benefit for you and you are living in the same household (see Appendix C for rates). Child Benefit counts as income and will be deducted in full when calculating entitlement to IS or JSA.

*Housing Benefit and Council Tax Benefit*

If your parents receive Housing Benefit and Council Tax Benefit they will get benefit for you during the CBEP – until you get a job or training place. Child Benefit counts as income for Housing Benefit and Council Tax Benefit purposes when entitlement to these two payments is calculated.

*Family Credit*

You will count as a dependant for the purposes of Family Credit only if, at the date of the claim, you are actually undergoing full-time, non-advanced education. You do not count as a dependant once you have actually left school even if your parents are still getting Child Benefit for you. Child Benefit does not count as income for Family Credit purposes and is not deducted when calculating entitlement to Family Credit.

## End of the CBEP

At the end of the CBEP if you have not got a job or YT place and are left without any income you may apply for discretionary JSA under the severe hardship provisions (see page 42).

# BRIDGING ALLOWANCE

Youth Training Bridging Allowance (YTBA) is an allowance awarded and paid by the Employment Service at the Jobcentre. You may be entitled to YTBA of £15 a week for up to eight weeks if you leave a job or YT outside of the CBEP, and under other circumstances if you are disabled. YTBA is designed to tide you over until you find another job or YT place. You must register with the Careers Service for YT.

If you have left a job it must have been paid employment (including self-employment and casual or temporary employment), undertaken between Monday and Friday, for more than 8 hours a week *(ES APG Ch 9, para 13)*.

YTBA is paid from the date of application at the Jobcentre. You must be registered at the Careers Service office. It is paid for a maximum of eight weeks (calculated as 40 week-days) in a period of 52 weeks. The 52-week period starts from the first day of payment. The allowance is a flat rate of £15 a week, calculated at £3 per day from Monday to Friday.

You can have left your job or YT for whatever reason and still be entitled to YTBA. But YTBA may be withdrawn if you refuse to accept a further offer of a YT place.

YTBA applicants do not have to actively seek employment or to be advised of a permitted period *(ESG 39, para G365)*.

## YTBA paid straight after CBEP

The YTBA will not normally be paid straight after the CBEP. However, it is available if you leave a job or YT place during the CBEP and your entitlement to Child Benefit expires in less than eight weeks. YTBA is payable for a period which brings the total payment of Child Benefit and YTBA to eight weeks. For example, if you leave your YT place six weeks before the end of the CBEP you will be entitled to Child Benefit for six weeks and YTBA for two weeks *(ES APG, Ch 9, para 7)*.

## YTBA paid when you have not been in a job or YT

To be eligible for YTBA, you will normally have left a job or YT place, unless one of the following applies:

✦ You were unable to have a job or go on YT during the CBEP – if, for example, you were sick or in custody *(ES APG, Ch 9, para 7)*.

✦ You could not look for a YT place during the CBEP because you were living abroad and your parents were entitled to receive Child Benefit on your behalf during the CBEP *(ES APG, Ch 9, para 7)*.

✦ You are disabled – see below.

### Living abroad

To receive 40 days YTBA you must have lived abroad during the CBEP and returned from abroad after the CBEP.

If you return from abroad near the end of the CBEP it may be possible to pay a balance of YTBA up to a maximum combined payment (Child Benefit and YTBA) of 40 days.

Most young people who come from abroad, including the European Union, are not eligible for YTBA on arrival in this country, even if they are eligible to join YT.

*Disability and YTBA*

If you are disabled you can receive YTBA without having left a job or YT place – you are eligible for YTBA for the length of time it takes you to find a suitable YT place or a job, or until the day before your 18th birthday, not just for eight weeks *(ES APG, Ch 9, paras 17,18)*.

The definition used comes from the Disability Discrimination Act 1995, which defines a disabled person as someone who has:

> "a physical or mental impairment which has a substantial and long term adverse effect on their ability to carry out normal day to day activities."

You will have to complete a form BA8 'Youth Training Bridging Allowance – Health Problems and Disabilities'. The ES check it and can then endorse your status. If there is a dispute about whether you are disabled, only a court or tribunal can decide *(ES APG, Ch 9, para 27)*.

## YTBA and JSA

You can claim JSA while you receive YTBA. If you do, YTBA is counted as income, which means that you do not benefit from receiving YTBA. However the current arrangement is that YTBA ceases once JSA is awarded. The exception is in the case of a discharged prisoner after the end of the CBEP, registered for YT, and living in board and lodgings, who can get YTBA and JSA at the same time for up to eight weeks *(ES APG, Ch 9, para 94)*. The YTBA is counted as income.

YTBA alone may not be considered enough income to support a young person *(JSA 16/17, Ch 7, para 38)*. If you have no other income you should make a claim for JSA either as someone who is entitled because they are in a prescribed group (see page 28) or under the severe hardship provisions (see page 42).

## YTBA and Housing Benefit

If you are living away from your family and have responsibility for paying rent you are eligible for Housing Benefit while you are on YTBA. You should claim this from your local authority. You should also make a claim for JSA.

## Credits of National Insurance contributions

Class 1 credits of NI contributions are not awarded to under 18s on YTBA. People under 18 are automatically awarded Class 3 credits up to and including the year of their 18th birthday.

## To claim YTBA

To claim YTBA you should register with the Careers Service and pick up the form BA1. You need to complete sections A, B and C; the office should fill in section D. Take the completed BA1 to the local Jobcentre, where your claim will be processed.

If you qualify for YTBA you must attend the Jobcentre fortnightly to sign. YTBA is paid fortnightly in arrears by Giro or by Automatic Credit Transfer to a bank account. In certain circumstances young people with disabilities or living in areas with poor transport facilities can claim YTBA by post.

If you attend the Jobcentre more than two days after you registered with the Careers Service you will be asked for an explanation. If the reason given is acceptable (e.g. you were looking for work or training or there was an illness in the family), then you will be paid from the date of initial registration. If the reason given is unacceptable then you will be interviewed by a supervisor who will explain that the allowance will be paid only from the date of the claim at the Jobcentre rather than the initial registration with the Careers Service. You will still be eligible for 40 days of YTBA.

Similar rules apply for late signing. If your fortnightly application is not made on the allocated 'signing day', your record is put on 'hold' and you will be asked for an explanation. If the reason given is not acceptable, the Jobcentre will stop YTBA for the period in question. After five days of non-attendance your claim is terminated.

## Whilst on YTBA

To be eligible for YTBA, you must apply for a YT place, make yourself available for interviews when required and be prepared to start on a YT course at any time.

### Holidays

If you go on holiday and state that you are not available to accept a YT place during the holiday period, YTBA should not be paid for any days that you say that you will be or have been on holiday. You can get YTBA if *(ES APG, Ch 9, para 81)*:

✦ you are not going abroad; and

✦ you offer to be available for YT whilst on holiday; and

✦ you sign a statement with a contact address saying you are willing to return for a YT place or interview.

### Sickness

If you are sick you will no longer be eligible for YTBA and will be referred to the local Benefits Agency office where you may be able to claim Incapacity Benefit or IS.

### Part-time education

You can receive YTBA if you attend college on a part-time basis providing you *(ES APG, Ch 9, para 76)*:

✦ satisfy the normal eligibility rules;

✦ sign a written statement that you are willing to give up your studies to take up a training opportunity;

✦ are available to attend interviews on the days you normally study.

*Part-time work*

To receive YTBA for any day, you have to have been available on that day to attend an interview for YT or take up a YT place. Any part-time work done outside the usual hours for the type of employment for which you are seeking training (e.g. 9 a.m. – 5 p.m. Monday to Friday) will not affect your entitlement to YTBA.

You can get YTBA for any day when you work part-time and offer to sign a statement saying that you are *(ES APG, Ch 9, para 75)*:
✦ willing to give up the employment to take up a training opportunity; and
✦ available to attend training interviews on the days you normally work.

## Termination of YTBA

The Jobcentre will notify you and the Careers Service 20 days before the YTBA is due to end. When the last payment of YTBA is made, you will be sent a letter saying that YTBA can no longer be paid. If relevant, it will give a future date from which a new application for YTBA can be accepted.

In all cases YTBA will stop:
✦ after 40 days of payment; or
✦ if you find work or enter YT before 40 days of payment; or
✦ if you successfully claim JSA; or
✦ the day before your 18th birthday (after which you can claim JSA if you are still unemployed); or
✦ if you refuse a suitable YT place without good cause; or
✦ if you fail to attend the Jobcentre.

## Refusal of a suitable YT place

When you apply for YTBA, you have to sign this declaration on form BA1:

> "I understand that I must be prepared to accept an offer of a suitable place on Youth Training, and that payment of YT Bridging Allowance may be stopped if I refuse such an offer without good cause."

The only circumstance in which your entitlement to YTBA should be questioned is if you refuse a YT place and as a result are taken out of the Guarantee Group while you are receiving YTBA *(ES APG, Ch 9, para 107)*.

Having been notified of a refusal of a YT place by the Careers Service, the Jobcentre will refer your case to the Labour Market Adjudication Officer (LMAO) for consideration of 'Refusal of Training' (see page 54). The LMAO gives an 'opinion' on whether you would have been disallowed from receiving JSA if you were entitled to it, and can recommend that you be disqualified for between 1 and 26 weeks.

The steps to be followed in a case of refusing a suitable YT place are:
+ Careers officers notify the Jobcentre that you have refused to take up a YT place without good cause.
+ The Jobcentre stops paying YTBA (this should not apply to first-time entrants until the second refusal of a suitable YT place).
+ You are sent a copy of the report of refusal of training and invited to comment on it within 14 days.
+ If the case is straightforward, the Jobcentre takes a decision. If your response is reasonable they will pay YTBA.
+ If the case is not straightforward, it is referred to the LMAO for 'opinion only'.
+ The Jobcentre takes a decision on the basis of the LMAO's opinion.
+ The Jobcentre tells you of the decision and of how long the disqualification will last.
  *(ES APG Ch 9, para 108)*

If the proposed disqualification time goes beyond the end of YTBA entitlement, then you are disqualified for the whole YTBA period. YTBA is not suspended. Days disallowed count towards the 40 days' total *(ES APG Ch 9, para 118)*.

## Appeals

There is no *independent* appeals procedure against disqualification, but you can appeal against the decision to the Business Manager of the Jobcentre *(ES APG Ch 9 para 121)*. If you provide new evidence the appeal is referred back to the LMAO to review the original opinion. Otherwise the manager will decide whether or not to overturn the decision to disqualify you. Although LMAOs only give an 'opinion' in cases involving YTBA, they will still make their recommendation as if they were being asked to assess a claim for JSA.

## Requalifying for YTBA

Once you have used your full 40 days of YTBA you can requalify for YTBA only if:

✦ you have left YT, a Modern Apprenticeship or a job since you last received YTBA; **and**

✦ it is more than 52 weeks from the first day for which YTBA was paid.

If you have not got a YT place or a job by the end of the YTBA and are left without an income you may apply for JSA under the severe hardship provisions (see page 42).

# INCOME SUPPORT &
# JOBSEEKER'S ALLOWANCE

Some 16 and 17 year olds are eligible for benefits. They include young people who cannot work or go on YT, single parents, some young people who do not live with their parents and those who are sick.

In general, if you are claiming because you are unable to work you will claim Income Support (IS). If you are claiming because you have not yet found work or training you will claim Jobseeker's Allowance (JSA).

The age of entitlement for JSA is generally 18. However some 16 and 17 year olds can get it. Though the categories are limited **you should never be turned away from making a claim** *(JSA 16/17, Ch 3, para 2)*.

The categories of young people who are entitled are listed overleaf. For each category various additional conditions must be met. The categories and detailed conditions of entitlement are described in turn in the sections on IS and JSA which follow.

## IS

a) 16 and 17 year olds who can't work or go on a training course
b) Certain 16 and 17 year olds who are on a training course
c) Certain 16, 17 and 18 year olds in relevant education
d) Certain 16 and 17 year olds who are sick

## JSA

a) 16 and 17 year olds entitled to JSA during the CBEP
b) 16 and 17 year olds entitled to JSA for a limited time
c) 16 and 17 year olds entitled to JSA at any time
d) Those who get JSA under discretionary severe hardship provisions

---

**Prescribed groups**
Young people entitled to IS or JSA under any of these categories except the last (severe hardship applicants) are said to be in a **prescribed group**.

---

# INCOME SUPPORT

## Entitlement to IS

Although much IS has been replaced by JSA, IS still remains for people who are eligible without having to be available for work. IS can be paid on its own or, for some people, may be paid as a top-up to other benefits such as Incapacity Benefit or earnings from part-time work.

You can get IS at any time while you are 16 or 17 if you are in any of the following circumstances:

*a)* ***16 and 17 year olds who can't work or go on a training course*** *(IS (Gen) (JSA) Regs 1996 Sch 1B)*

✦ a single parent/single foster parent with a child under 16;

✦ looking after a child under 16 because the child's parent or the person who usually looks after the child is ill or temporarily away;

✦ looking after a member of the family who is temporarily ill;

✦ receiving Invalid Care Allowance;

✦ caring for someone who has claimed or gets Attendance Allowance or high or middle rate Disability Living Allowance;

✦ incapable of work;

✦ a disabled worker;

✦ a deaf or disabled student;

✦ registered blind;

✦ pregnant and incapable of work because of the pregnancy;

✦ expecting a baby in 11 weeks or less, or within seven weeks of having given birth – but not those in relevant education (unless included under another category);

✦ a 'person from abroad' entitled to benefit under the urgent cases regulations;

*continued ...*

✦ a refugee learning English on a course of more than 15 hours per week – you must have started the course within a year of arrival in Britain and you will be able to get IS for up to nine months;

✦ a member of a heterosexual couple looking after a child under 16 while the other member is temporarily out of the UK;

✦ appealing against a decision that you are not incapable of work;

✦ required to attend court.

*b)* ***Certain 16 and 17 year olds who are on a training course*** *(IS (Gen)(JSA) Regs Schedule 1B, para 28):*

✦ in receipt of a training allowance where it is lower than your IS entitlement, e.g. YT trainees who have children or are eligible for disability premium or living away from home for a good reason (see page 116 for trainees who can claim IS top-ups).

*c)* ***Certain 16, 17 and 18 year olds in relevant education*** *(IS (Gen) (JSA) Regs, Sch 1B, para 15; reg 13(2)(a)-(e))*

You can claim IS if you are in relevant education (see page 13 for definition of 'relevant') and in one of the following categories:

✦ you are a parent responsible for a child who lives in your household;

✦ you are so 'severely mentally or physically handicapped' that you would be unlikely to get a job in the next 12 months;

✦ you are an orphan with no-one **acting in place of your parents**;

✦ you are living away from your parents or any persons acting in place of your parents and they cannot support you as they are: ¶
  – chronically sick or mentally or physically disabled, or
  – in prison, or
  – unable to come to Britain because of the immigration laws;

✦ you are a refugee and have started to learn English (on a course or courses totalling more than 15 hours a week) in order to obtain employment, and started during your first year in Britain – you will be able to get IS for up to nine months;

*continued ...*

✦ you are of necessity living away from your parents or any persons acting in place of your parents because:
  – you are in **physical or moral danger**, or
  – you are **estranged** from your parents or any persons acting in their place, or
  – there is **serious risk to your physical or mental health**;
✦ you used to be in the local authority's care and of necessity are living away from your parents or any persons acting in place of your parents. Note: Care leavers in relevant education do not have to prove estrangement.

For phrases in **bold** and the item marked ¶, see notes under Definitions of terms, overleaf.

Your evidence should normally be accepted on the above. In cases of doubt additional evidence will be sought *(AOG, vol 4, para 25333)*. In cases of physical or moral danger, evidence from you or your representative should be accepted unless there is stronger evidence to the contrary *(AOG, vol 4, para 25336)*.

You are treated as being in relevant education until the end of the holiday after your last term – the terminal date (see page 13). So if you leave school during the Summer term, you will continue to be entitled to IS until September, or you can make your first claim during the summer holidays. In September you may be entitled to JSA under one of the other categories.

**Note:** If you are in Category (c) you can continue to claim IS until your 19th birthday; you do not need to claim JSA under the 16 hour rule. (See the *Unemployment and Training Rights Handbook* for more information on studying and claiming benefit – see page 149.)

### *d)  16 and 17 year olds who are sick*
   *(IS (Gen) (JSA) Regs 1996 Sch 1B, para 7)*
✦ If you are sick, have left school and your parents no longer get Child Benefit for you, you may get IS for as long as you are unable to work or go on a training course.

## Definitions of terms

The following guidance is given to Benefits Agency officers on the use of these terms:

### A person acting in the place of your parents

In deciding whether a person is acting in place of your parents, consideration should to be given to such factors as whether the person *(AOG, vol 6, para 35554):*

◆ provides supervision and financial, social, moral or other care and guidance;

◆ provides shelter, food and clothing;

◆ is responsible for any necessary disciplinary action;
  as would be appropriate for a person the same age as you.

A person acting in the place of your parents includes:

◆ a local authority or voluntary organisation where, under a relevant enactment,
  - in England and Wales the claimant is being looked after by them; or
  - in Scotland is in their care; and
  - can include the person with whom you are placed (in Scotland, boarded), whether or not payment is made.

◆ (only for young people in the category marked ¶ above) the person with whom you are placed (in Scotland, boarded) irrespective of who made the arrangements.

### In physical or moral danger

In physical or moral danger will apply if you would be in such danger if you lived at home The danger does not have to come from your parents. If you or your representative submits that you would be in physical or moral danger this should be accepted unless there is 'stronger evidence to the contrary'. But you will not satisfy this provision unless you are able to show that you have **of necessity** to live away from home because of it *(AOG, vol 4, para 25336).*

*continued...*

**Estranged**

Estranged is given its dictionary meaning of 'alienated in feeling or affection'. It may be decided that you are estranged from your parents if you have neither the intention nor the wish to live with them and no wish to have any prolonged physical or emotional association with them, or if they feel similarly towards you. There may be estrangement even where your parents are providing some financial support. However you will not satisfy this provision just because you say you are estranged. You must also show you have **of necessity** to live away from your parents because of the estrangement *(AOG, vol 4, para 25335)*.

**Serious risk to physical or mental health**

The fact that there may be a risk to your health will not be enough to include you in this category. There must be a **serious risk to physical or mental health**. This could apply if, for example, you suffer from chronic bronchitis which is aggravated by the damp conditions in your parents' home or you have a history of mental illness which is aggravated by your parents' attitude towards you *(AOG, vol 4, para 25337)*. You must also show that because of the serious risk you have **of necessity** to live away from home.

## How to claim IS

Either go to your local Benefits Agency office or contact the office by phone or letter, and ask for a form A1. You should complete, sign and return the form within one month of first contacting the Benefits Agency office. This means the claim will be accepted from the date of first contact. An adjudication officer decides if you can be paid IS. You will get a letter telling you what they decide. Payment can be made by girocheque or order book cashable at a Post Office of your choice, or by Automatic Credit Transfer into an account of your choice.

# JOBSEEKER'S ALLOWANCE

## Entitlement to JSA

There are two types of JSA:

♦ contributory JSA, which has replaced Unemployment Benefit;

♦ means-tested (or 'income-based' or 'income-related' JSA), which has replaced IS for claimants who have to be available for work.

Contributory JSA is paid to people who have worked and paid enough National Insurance contributions. Very few 16 and 17 year olds will qualify. The rest of this section is about income-based JSA.

### a) 16 and 17 year olds eligible to claim JSA during the CBEP

Certain young people who are married or living away from home during the CBEP can claim JSA in their own right. You can claim JSA for this limited period of time, so long as you have registered for a YT place, if you *(JSA Regs, reg 57)*:

♦ are married and your partner is one of the following:
  - 18 or over,
  - 16/17 and registered for work and training,
  - a young person eligible for JSA/IS,
  - a young person who is a member of a couple and is responsible for a child in the household,
  - a young person laid off or on short time for up to 13 weeks who is available for employment,
  - a young person temporarily absent from GB because they are taking their child abroad for treatment,
  - a young person incapable of work and training because of severe mental or physical disability or disease which medical advice says is unlikely to end within 12 months;

*continued ...*

✦ have no living parent and no-one acting in the place of a parent (see page 32);

✦ are not living with a parent or any person acting in the place of a parent and you:
  – were in custody or in local authority care immediately before your 16th birthday, or
  – were placed away from home as part of a programme of resettlement or rehabilitation under the supervision of a probation officer or social worker, or
  – are living away from home to avoid physical or sexual abuse (your word should be accepted on this unless there is other evidence which casts doubt on it *(AOG, vol 6, para 35624))*, or
  – have to live away from home because you need other accommodation because of a mental illness or mental or physical disability;

✦ are living away from your parents' or guardians' home and they are unable to support you financially as they are:
  – in custody, or
  – chronically sick or mentally or physically disabled, or
  – outside Great Britain and prohibited from entering or re-entering the country (this includes those whose parents are unable to come to this country because of Britain's immigration rules);

✦ are **of necessity** living away from your parents or any persons acting in place of your parents because:
  – you are estranged (see page 33) from them, or
  – you are in physical or moral danger (see page 32), or
  – there is serious risk to your physical or mental health (see page 33).

---

**Good reasons for living away from home**

All the items in the above list except the first one are referred to in this Guide as **'good reasons' for living away from home**.

---

## b)  16 and 17 year olds entitled to JSA for a limited time

There are some circumstances in which you will be entitled to eight weeks of JSA. They are if you *(JSA Regs, reg 60)*:

✦ have been discharged from custody after the CBEP and have good reason to live independently (the same 'good reasons' as in (a) above).

✦ have stopped living in accommodation provided by the local authority under Part III of the Children Act 1989 and are of necessity living away from your parents or anyone acting in their place. You will be entitled whether you leave during or after the CBEP.

If you have just left custody or are a local authority accommodation leaver you are entitled to JSA for up to eight weeks or until your 18th birthday or until you find a job or YT place, whichever is first. JSA will stop after eight weeks, even if you haven't found a YT place, unless you become eligible under another category.

## c)  16 and 17 year olds eligible for income-based JSA at any time

You will be entitled to JSA at any time if you *(JSA Regs, reg 61)*:

✦ have been temporarily laid off work or put on short-time – for a maximum of 13 weeks;

✦ are a member of a couple who is held to be responsible for a child;

✦ would be entitled to claim IS but decide to claim income-based JSA (an adult might do this in order to get NI contribution credits, but there is no obvious advantage for a young person);

✦ have accepted a firm offer of a job in the Armed Forces and:
  – were not in employment or training at the time of the offer, and
  – have never had a reduction of income-based JSA because of an employment or training sanction (except for Jobseeker's Direction), and
  – have accepted an enlistment date not more than eight weeks after the offer was made.

## d) Severe hardship payments

If you don't fall into any of the above groups and you have little or no money you can still make a claim for JSA. JSA should be paid if severe hardship will result unless it is paid *(JS Act 95, Section 16(1))*. Technically the payment is made at the discretion of the Secretary of State. In practice, decisions are made on the Secretary of State's behalf either by the local Jobcentre or by the Severe Hardship Claims Unit (SHCU) in Glasgow.

You should only be considered under Severe Hardship provision if you cannot get JSA in any other way *(JSA 16/17, Ch 4, para 6)*.

---

**What is 'severe hardship'?**

Severe hardship is not defined in the regulations and there are no official rules published by the DSS or Benefits Agency. However the following are considered *(JSA 16/17, Ch 10, para 2)*:

✦ accommodation, and the risk of losing any accommodation if JSA were not paid;

✦ means of support, including any income or savings, and anyone else who could support you;

✦ health and vulnerability.

**These are only guidelines. Whatever your circumstances, if you believe you are suffering hardship you should apply for JSA and your case should be looked at.**

---

More than 80% of those who apply for severe hardship payments are successful.

All cases are looked at individually and you should mention all the factors which you think are relevant to your case. Payments have been paid to young people, for example:

✦ who have been unable to find a YT place by the end of their CBEP, or by the end of the eight weeks covered by the YTBA;

✦ who are on YTBA but where £15 is not enough to prevent severe hardship – if a severe hardship payment is made in these cases, YTBA will stop being paid unless the young person is a discharged prisoner (see page 21);

✦ who are living with family or friends who cannot or will not support them financially because, for example, relationships have broken down or they are on benefits themselves or in low paid work.

The system for claiming these payments is described on pages 42–51.

# How to claim JSA

You will be required actively to look for work and training. Training includes Youth Training, Modern Apprenticeships and National Traineeships. You can also look for a job with training, and for a full-time education opportunity.

There is a three-day waiting period after you claim before you can get JSA, unless you are claiming it under severe hardship provision.

If you have entitlement to Bridging Allowance (YTBA) and wish to claim YTBA only, you will have form BA1 from the Careers Service. YTBA is not part of JSA. If you wish to claim YTBA and JSA, the YTBA claim should be dealt with first.

## Registering with the Careers Service

You do not need to register with the Careers Service if you are:
+ claiming contribution-based JSA – you claim on the same basis as adults and the special rules for young people do not apply to you;
+ temporarily laid off work;
+ waiting to take up a place in the Armed Forces.

You do not have to register with the Careers Service immediately if:
+ the Careers Service is affected by an emergency, e.g. a fire or a strike;
+ there is not enough time to visit the Careers Service and get back to the Jobcentre before it closes and you would suffer hardship is your claim was delayed.

In these circumstances you can register with the ES and then register at the Careers Service within a limited time. Your claim will be for a limited period *(JSA 16/17, Ch 3, para 9)*.

In all other cases you need to register with the Careers Service for training and employment. Take proof of registration to the local Jobcentre. Proof of registration is a referral form ES9 or an emergency referral form ES11.

*Forms and information for the Jobseeker's Interview*

Take to the Jobcentre your National Insurance (NI) number, if you have one, and your P45 from your last job, if you have one.

If you do not have a National Insurance number, your claim should not be delayed while it is allocated *(JSA 16/17, Ch 3, para 12)*.

The Jobcentre should give you the JSA claim form, JSA1, and a 'Finding a Job or Training' form, ES6. You should complete these forms before the interview if you have time. If not, or if you have difficulty completing the forms, you can get help when the forms are checked before your interview *(JSA 16/17, Ch 3, para 16)*.

If you need your Careers Service referral form ES9 to help you complete the forms, you should be given it back *(JSA 16/17, Ch 3, para 16)*.

*The interview*

Interviews should be carried out by trained specialists with good interviewing skills and the ability to handle sensitive issues *(JSA 16/17, Ch 5, para 1)*.

*Jobseeker's Agreement*

Young people have a special Jobseeker's Agreement, form ES7. The difference from the adult one is in its references to training. It should be drawn up in discussion with you. It will take into account information from your ES9 (Careers Service referral form) and your ES6 ('Finding a Job or Training' form) *(JSA 16/17, Ch 2, para 14; Ch 5, para 21)*.

The Jobseeker's Agreement lists *(JSA 16/17, Ch 5, para 31)*:
✦ your availability for work, including any restrictions;
✦ the type of work and training you are looking for;
✦ the activities you will carry out each week to look for work and training and improve your chances of finding them;
✦ what the ES will do to help you;
✦ brief information on sanctions and disallowances.

You keep a copy of your Jobseeker's Agreement *(JSA 16/17, Cb 5, para 47)*.

If you do not sign the agreement, or cannot agree with the ES Adviser on what should be in it, your case will be referred to adjudication *(JSA 16/17, Cb 5, para 34)*.

There are various circumstances in which you may be **sanctioned** while receiving JSA (for details see pages 53 to 58).

If you have not been sanctioned you have certain '**labour market concessions**'. You can restrict your availability to training and jobs with suitable training *(JSA 16/17, Cb 5, para 39)*. You can refuse jobs which do not offer suitable training *(JSA 16/17, Cb 2, para 11)*. A Jobseeker's Direction does not count as a sanction for this purpose *(JSA 16/17, Cb 5, para 45)*.

'Suitable' training is defined in the same way as for YT, that is taking into account *(AOG Vol 6, para 39871)*:
✦ your personal capacity;
✦ your aptitude;
✦ your preference;
✦ employer's preference;
✦ the level of approved qualification aimed at;
✦ the duration of training;
✦ proximity;
✦ prompt availability.

If you have not been sanctioned you must actively seek work and training. You can also include steps to find full-time education in your search activities. You must take at least one step each week to find work and one to find training. If it is reasonable in a particular week to take only one step, it can be either to find work or training *(JSA 16/17, Cb 5, para 42)*.

If you have been sanctioned you lose labour market concessions. That is, you may be penalised if you restrict your availability to training and jobs with suitable training or if you refuse jobs which do not offer suitable training. You must actively seek work. You can look for training and full-time education as a step to getting work *(JSA 16/17, Ch 5, para 40)*.

*Jobseeker's Direction*

This is a written statement given to you telling you what you must do to improve your chance of getting a job.

If you have 'labour market concessions' (e.g. the right to refuse employment without suitable training, see page 41), you must not be directed to do something which contradicts the concession *(JSA 16/17, Ch 16, para 9)*. For this reason the Careers Service should be consulted before the Jobseeker's Direction is issued.

# Claiming severe hardship payments

Severe hardship can be considered during a new jobseeker interview. The decision on whether to pay under the severe hardship provision is made on behalf of the Secretary of State by a Jobcentre officer. This officer must have completed the Severe Hardship Direction training package and hold a Certificate of Authority from the SHCU in Glasgow. Combining the role of interviewing officer and certificated officer makes the process quicker and more efficient *(JSA 16/17, Ch 7, para 7)*.

If no one with the certificate is present the case can be referred to the SHCU. Refusals and borderline cases must be referred to the SHCU in any case.

The certificated officer at the Jobcentre can decide to pay you JSA under the severe hardship provisions, but they cannot decide to refuse a payment – only the SHCU can make a decision to refuse payment.

The certified officer is responsible for *(JSA 16/17, Ch 6, para 4)*:
+ deciding if you would suffer severe hardship if no payment were made;
+ making directions to pay JSA; and
+ deciding on the length of the direction.

The following cases must be referred to SHCU *(JSA 16/17, Ch 7 para 43)*:
+ all cases if an 'authorised officer' is not available;
+ likely refusals;
+ sensitive or borderline cases;
+ likely revocations (see page 50);
+ where a care order is currently in force;
+ if you are living with a partner;
+ if payment is not appropriate from the date of claim;
+ if back-dating because of good cause is appropriate;
+ if severe hardship payments have been made for 16 weeks continuously and you have remained registered for training and employment throughout that period;
+ if you have not registered for YT after a 'short-term direction' (to make a severe hardship payment) has expired;
+ when permission to contact parents/third parties is refused without good reason;
+ in alleged abuse cases when a referral to Social Services is refused without good reason.

The Benefits Agency adjudication officer decides *(JSA 16/17, Ch 6, para 5)*:
+ the date of claim;
+ whether there is entitlement under a prescribed group;
+ the rate of JSA payable; and
+ entitlement reflecting ES adjudication on fulfilment of labour market conditions.

You can appeal against decisions made by adjudication officers *(JSA 16/17, Ch 6, para 7)*.

## Severe hardship interviews

Interviewers are asked to 'Remember that many young people are very vulnerable because of the circumstances leading to the claim' *(JSA 16/17, Ch 7, para 3)*.

The Jobcentre should let someone accompany you at the interview so long as s/he is not disruptive or unhelpful. You should have the opportunity to ask him/her to leave if you want to *(JSA 16/17, Ch 7, para 4)*.

Only information needed to decide on your claim must be sought. Information that will allow you to be traced must not be released without your permission *(JSA 16/17, Ch 7, para 10)*.

The interviewer has a pro forma listing the information that s/he needs to obtain from you. This includes the items shown in Box 1.

| **Box 1. Information collected at severe hardship interviews** | |
|---|---|
| **Claim details** | Date of claim, name, address, date of birth, NI number, date you left relevant education.<br>Details of partner, if any.<br>What you have been doing since leaving school or since your last claim for benefit.<br>Details of last employment and earnings, including what you spent it on if spent.<br>Are you supported by relatives or friends?<br>Have you ever been in custody?<br>Benefit payments.<br>Have you ever been in care and are you still the subject of a care order?<br>Are you living with parents or guardian?<br>   If yes, why can't they support you?<br>   If no, why aren't you living with them?<br>When did you leave home?<br>Can you return home?<br>Can you return home and be supported financially? |
| | *continued ...* |

| **Box 1 continued** | |
|---|---|
| **Accommodation details** | Type of accommodation and cost. Do you have access to cooking facilities? Have you applied for Housing Benefit? Will you have to pay any money to the landlord over and above HB? Is there any risk of eviction if JSA is not paid? |
| **Financial circumstances** | Are you getting/have you applied for YTBA? Do you or your partner have any other income? Any savings? How much? Any debts? Type? How much? Any deductions from benefit payable at present? Any relatives or friends who can help? |
| **Health matters** | Are you/your partner pregnant? If yes, expected date of delivery? Do you or your partner have any health problem? |
| **Miscellaneous** | Are you represented by a third party? If so, type of representative (e.g. social worker, friend, relative)? **Why do you think you are in hardship?** |
| *Condensed from: JSA 16/17, Appendix 18* | |

## Third party evidence

The interviewer must ask your permission before contacting your parents, or a third party, who can confirm what you say. If you refuse without good reason they will explain that there may not be enough evidence to pay you JSA under the severe hardship provision. However the interviewer must not put 'undue pressure' on you to give permission for them to contact your parents or another third party. Your consent 'must be given voluntarily and not as a result of threats or inducements' *(JSA 16/17, Ch 7, para 8)*.

If you refuse permission without good reason or your parents or the third party are not available, the interviewer will ask you to get written confirmation from them of what you have said. If you don't, the case will be referred to the SHCU.

If your parents or another third party cannot respond because they are on holiday or not immediately available, you might get short-term payments for up to two weeks if you would otherwise suffer severe hardship, such as eviction.

If you are accompanied by a 'responsible third party such as an adult relative, social worker or recognised voluntary worker', they will be asked to confirm your evidence. Outside organisations, or someone like a youth or advice worker, may be able to offer evidence to support what you say. Evidence can be presented in person, by telephone or in writing *(JSA 16/17, Ch 7, paras 15-18)*. Evidence from a responsible third party may mean that contact with your parents is not necessary.

## If you are not living with your parents

If you are living independently, the interviewer will record the reasons and ask if it is possible to return home. S/he will ask permission to contact your parents, or a third party, who can confirm what you say, and explain that if you refuse without good reason there may not be enough evidence to pay you JSA under the severe hardship provision. However the interviewer must not put undue pressure on you to agree *(JSA 16/17, Ch 7, para 26)*.

If you are married you are not subject to any checks on whether your parents could support you.

If you have come from the Republic of Ireland and your parents are there, you will be questioned about estrangement. If your parents cannot be contacted by telephone, your evidence should be accepted.

If you have come from abroad, including the EU, and your parents are still there it will not usually be necessary to contact them, but the Habitual Residence Test will be considered (see page 67).

If you are staying in a bail or probation hostel as a condition of the court you will not have to return to your parents.

If you were the subject of a care order it will not normally be necessary to contact your parents. Social services should confirm that they are not supporting you.

If evidence from both you and your parent needs to be considered to decide whether you are unable to live at home, and if the evidence is contradictory and equally balanced, you must be given the benefit of the doubt *(16/17 News and Views, SHCU, BA, September 1995)*.

### If you are living with your parents

You can be living with your parents or guardians and still be in severe hardship *(JSA 16/17, Ch 8, para 19)*.

The interviewer will want details of your parents' circumstances.

If a parent has been supporting you before your claim, the interviewer will want to know what has changed that prevents your parent continuing to support you. Your parents' income and outgoings do not need to be verified by bank statements or bills.

If a parent refuses to support you – to provide sufficient food and shelter – and verifies this either verbally or in writing then Jobcentre staff should consider hardship payments *(16/17 News and Views, SHCU, BA, September 1995).*

If you are on YTBA and your parents are prepared to support you as long as you contribute some of it towards your keep, Jobcentre staff are unlikely to think there is a risk of severe hardship.

## Suspected abuse

If the interviewer suspects serious abuse or the risk of it, s/he will inform social services and the police. S/he will ask your permission first, but may go ahead even if you don't give it. This is the only situation in which information can be passed to social services etc. without your permission *(JSA 16/17, Ch 7, para 28).*

If you say you have been abused, you will be asked *(JSA 16/17, para 29):*
- ✦ about the kind of abuse – e.g. physical, sexual, or emotional;
- ✦ how long it has been going on;
- ✦ whether there are any other children or young people living in the family home;
- ✦ if you have not already got a social worker, whether you would like to be referred to social services for help and advice;
- ✦ if you have got a social worker, whether can they be contacted to confirm your reasons for claiming.

The interviewer must not probe further than the above questions *(JSA 16/17, Ch 7, para 30).*

S/he must not put undue pressure on you to attend social services. Your attendance must be voluntary and not a result of threats or inducements *(JSA 16/17, Ch 7, para 32).* If you agree to a referral to social services, the interviewer will try to arrange an appointment for you, and will give you short-term severe hardship payments in the meantime *(JSA 16/17, Ch 7, para 31).*

## The payment system

Severe hardship payments are paid at the same rate as any other payments of JSA (see page 52 and Appendix C).

The period for which you will be awarded JSA under the severe hardship provisions will depend on your circumstances and how long the Jobcentre officer believes it is likely to take you to find a YT place.

Initial payments are usually made for eight weeks.

Shorter payments are usually made if you are in a priority group for early placement in YT because you are sleeping rough, pregnant, a young offender or a care leaver. If you are in this group, your TEC or LEC will be asked to investigate and assist in finding you a YT place after six weeks instead of eight weeks.

Awards can be made for up to 16 weeks if any of the following changes are expected to occur within that time *(JSA 16/17, Ch 9, para 19)*:
◆ you will reach your 18th birthday;
◆ you are pregnant and will be within 11 weeks of the expected birth;
◆ you will start a training course or work;
◆ you will start further education.

You will be paid in arrears. If you need money urgently you should apply for a Social Fund crisis loan (see page 64). This will have to be repaid.

During the period of the award the ES will check regularly with the Careers Service that you are still looking for a YT place. You will be asked to attend the Jobcentre for an interview if, for example, you are not attending the Careers Service office regularly, being restrictive about the YT you are willing to consider, deliberately failing YT interviews or not keeping appointments or interviews.

Your TEC or LEC will be asked to investigate and assist in finding you a YT placement if you have not found a YT place after eight weeks, or after six weeks if you are *(JSA 16/17, Ch 16, para 8):*

✦ a young offender;
✦ pregnant;
✦ sleeping rough;
✦ a care leaver.

## Revocation of directions

Your payments can be stopped early (revoked) if:

✦ your circumstances have changed so you are no longer at risk of severe hardship;
✦ you have, without 'good cause', failed to pursue an opportunity of training or rejected an offer of training (see page 54);
✦ the original severe hardship direction was based on a mistake of fact, or ignorance of a fact.

Revocations can only be made by the SHCU. If you want to re-claim you will have to have a full new claim interview.

If you stop satisfying basic labour market entitlement conditions – such as attending the careers office and the Jobcentre as required, being available for and actively seeking work – you can cease to be entitled to payments. This decision is made locally by the labour market adjudication officer. You have a right of appeal.

## Repeat claims

Severe hardship payments are made for a fixed period of time. If payment is due to stop and you still do not have a training place or job and your circumstances have not changed, you should apply again.

The Jobcentre will interview you to review your circumstances.

The Careers Service will be contacted to ask for the same information as at the time of the original claim.

## Appeals

You *cannot* appeal against a decision made on behalf of the Secretary of State, i.e. on whether to pay JSA under severe hardship provision or the period for which it is payable. However, you can make further representations if you feel that the Secretary of State or his officer has not taken into account all the relevant factors. Local offices should review the decision if there has been an error of fact or information they did not previously take into account.

You *can* appeal against decisions made by an adjudication officer (AO). AO decisions include the amount of JSA payable and entitlement to JSA under categories other than severe hardship – e.g. if you are applying during the CBEP on the grounds of estrangement (see pages 34 to 36).

If, after you apply, your circumstances change, e.g. the friends you are staying with ask you to leave, you should apply again, even if you have only just been turned down.

# IS/JSA rates

Current rates of benefit are given in Appendix C.

## Single people

There are two rates of personal allowance for 16/17 year olds, £38.90 and £29.60 (1997/98 rates). The higher rate (the same rate as paid to 18-24 year olds), is paid to a young person who is entitled to IS *(IS (Gen) Regs Sch 2)* or JSA *(JSA Regs, Sch 1, para 1)* and:

◆ is eligible for **disability premium**; or
◆ is seen to have a **good reason** for living away from home (see page 34).

The higher rate can be claimed whenever there is entitlement to IS or JSA, both during and after the CBEP.

Always check whether you are entitled to get the higher rate as it has not always been automatically given.

Gay couples are treated as single claimants.

## Heterosexual couples

If either partner of a heterosexual couple is under the age of 18, both must separately establish entitlement to JSA in order to receive the full couple rate. If only one of you can establish entitlement to JSA then as a couple you will receive the appropriate single person's allowance, taking account of the age of the person who claims.

# Sanctions and reductions in JSA

Sanctions and reductions in JSA differ depending on:
+ whether you were in work or training;
+ the route by which you are claiming JSA (prescribed group or severe hardship);
+ whether you are a new jobseeker;
+ whether you refused an opportunity or left one voluntarily/ prematurely;
+ whether you left because of misconduct.

When you first leave full-time education you are a **new jobseeker**. You stop being a new jobseeker if you *(JSA 16/17, Ch 2 para 15)*:
+ take up employment or self-employment for 16 hours or more a week;
+ complete a course of training;
+ fail to complete a course of training without a certificate to show good cause applied (young people in severe hardship);
+ give up a training place without good cause (all young people);
+ lose a training place through misconduct (all young people).

## New jobseekers

As a new jobseeker, you can fail to apply for or accept, refuse, fail to attend, fail to pursue, neglect to avail yourself of or leave **one** training place voluntarily without **good cause** without incurring a sanction. You are regarded this one time as having 'automatic good cause'.

If you fail to apply for or accept, refuse, fail to attend, fail to pursue, neglect to avail yourself of or leave a training place **with** good cause, then you are still a new jobseeker. In other words, you should not be sanctioned for doing one of these things without good cause on **one** subsequent occasion *(JSA 16/17, Ch 2 para 16,17)*.

However, sanctions will apply if you:
+ leave a **job voluntarily** or through **misconduct**; or
+ do not complete **training** because of **misconduct.**

# 'Good cause'

## Training

If you refuse, fail to attend, neglect to avail yourself of or leave a place on YT (with non-employed status), consideration must be given to any potential good cause. The following are good causes *(JSA Regs, reg 73)*:

✦ a disease or bodily or mental disablement that meant you were not able to attend, or that attending would have put your health at risk, or the health or other people at risk *(AOG, vol 6, para 39766);*

✦ a sincere religious or conscientious objection *(AOG, vol 6, para 39769);*

✦ caring responsibilities when no close relative or other member of the person's household was available to care for them and it was not practical to make other arrangements *(AOG, vol 6, 39772)* – but your availability/actively seeking employment may be questioned;

✦ attendance at court;

✦ arranging or attending a funeral;

✦ the time it normally takes to travel to the place of training or back is more than an hour, unless there was no appropriate training scheme available within one hour;

✦ you had to deal with a domestic emergency – the nature of the emergency will be considered, and your availability for/actively seeking work may be questioned.

### *Refusing YT while undertaking other training*

If you are undertaking part-time study to help your employment prospects or advance your career, you will usually have good cause for refusing a YT place *(AOG, vol 6, para 39811)*. But the type of course and hours of attendance will be taken into account. If you are attending college for only a few hours per week in preparation for retaking failed examinations and you could attend classes in the evening you will not be seen to have good cause for refusing to participate in YT. You do have good cause, however, if you have to attend college frequently to complete a specific course which will improve your chances of getting work.

However, note that other training may put your availability for employment, and hence your eligibility for JSA, into doubt.

*Leaving substandard training*
If you leave YT because you think your training is substandard, a decision on good cause may depend on how you handled the situation.

Good cause should be accepted if *(AOG, vol 6, para 39800):*
◆ the agreed training programme was not being followed;
◆ you tried to resolve the problem by a reasonable approach to:
 – the YT provider involved, or
 – the Careers Service, or
 – the TEC/LEC, or
 – the ES District Manager or local Jobcentre

For more details on leaving YT because of substandard training, see page 95.

## Employment

The following are good cause for refusing or failing to apply for or neglecting to avail yourself of a job *(JSA Regs, reg 72):*
◆ it would cause significant harm to your health or subject you to excessive physical or mental stress;
◆ a sincere religious or conscientious objection;
◆ caring responsibilities made it unreasonable;
◆ excessive travelling time;
◆ unreasonably high expenses.

## Not a new jobseeker

If you are **not a new jobseeker** the following sanctions and reductions apply:

### *Leaving voluntarily or through misconduct*

If you leave **employment** (including employed-status training) **voluntarily** or through **misconduct** you are sanctioned in the same way as an adult and the case is referred to adjudication in the same way as an adult case. Your JSA can be stopped for between 1 and 26 weeks. JSA is not suspended while waiting for the decision.

You can apply for payments under the JSA hardship provision in certain circumstances (see page 60).

If you were unemployed for 13 weeks and then took a job, there is a 'trial period' from the fifth to the 12th week when you can leave for any reason other than misconduct, without incurring sanctions *(JS Act 95, 20(3), JS Regs, reg 74)*. This is called Employment on Trial.

If you leave **training** (non-employed status) **voluntarily** without good cause and claim JSA as a member of a **prescribed group** (see page 28), you will be sanctioned by having your JSA reduced for a set period of two weeks. It will be reduced by 40%, or 20% if you or a member of your family is seriously ill or pregnant.

If you leave **training voluntarily** without good cause and claim JSA on grounds of **severe hardship**, your JSA will automatically be reduced for two weeks by 40%, or 20% if you are seriously ill or pregnant.

### *Refusal of or neglect to avail*

If you refuse or neglect to avail yourself of **employment** (including employed-status training) you can be sanctioned unless you still have your 'labour market concession'*(JSA 16/17, Ch 16, para 12)*. This is a right to refuse jobs which do not offer suitable training, which you usually have if you have not previously been sanctioned (see page 41).

Your JSA will be reduced for two weeks, or until your 18th birthday if that is sooner.

The ES or the Careers Service must have offered you the job.

If you refuse **training** (not employed-status) and you are claiming JSA as a member of a **prescribed group** your JSA can be reduced by 40% or 20% for two weeks.

If you refuse **training** and you are claiming JSA on grounds of **severe hardship**, your payments can be revoked (stopped). If you make a new claim, your payments will be reduced by 40% or 20% for the first two weeks.

Employed-status training counts as employment.

## Decisions on good cause

*Prescribed groups*

For prescribed groups, cases of refusal or premature termination of training or leaving because of misconduct are decided by adjudication. If you leave a place, you will get a form ES86Y to state the reasons why you left. If misconduct is involved, the training provider will be asked for information.

*Severe hardship claimants*

If you are claiming JSA on grounds of severe hardship, such cases are not determined by adjudication. The ES Adviser, on behalf of the Secretary of State, decides whether you had good cause. If you had good cause to leave training, a certificate of good cause will be issued.

If you **refuse a place** the Careers Service notifies the ES on form ES 195T. This should be checked for evidence from you that you think establishes good cause. If more evidence is required, you should be invited to explain your refusal at an interview at the Jobcentre as soon as possible. If you do not attend, it will be assumed you do not wish to comment.

If the ES does not consider there was good cause, payment is automatically reduced for the first two weeks of your new claim for JSA.

If you **fail to complete a training course**, the ES Adviser will decide whether you had good cause, after considering evidence from the Careers Service and from you. If s/he decides that there is good cause, a certificate ES91 will be issued and a copy given to you. A good cause certificate will be issued whether the good cause was actual or 'automatic', i.e. you were a new jobseeker with a right to one 'training offence'. (See page 95 for the procedures followed if you leave a training course which you believe to be substandard.)

If the ES Adviser decides that there was not good cause, or if there was misconduct, you should get a Decision Certificate ES92 and your payments will be reduced by 40% or 20% for two weeks *(JSA 16/17, Ch 16, paras 39-44)*.

## Misconduct

It is up to the person who alleges you committed misconduct to prove it – usually the Training Provider. For the ES Adviser to decide you committed misconduct, there must be a high probability that the allegations against you are true *(JSA 16/17, Ch 16, para 46)*.

## What is misconduct?

Misconduct is not defined in regulations. It is blameworthy and wrong conduct, connected directly or indirectly to your activities on the training course *(JSA 16/17, Ch 16, para 51-2)*.

The following are **not** misconduct *(JSA 16/17, Ch 16, para 53,54)*:
◆ refusal to do work that is not part of the training agreement;
◆ refusing to work overtime if it is not explicitly mentioned in the training agreement, or if the request is not reasonable or adequate notice is not given;
◆ inefficiency if you were doing your best – inefficiency can only be misconduct where you are failing to meet standards within your capabilities;
◆ cases in which there is medical evidence that you were not responsible for your actions due to mental illness;
◆ cases in which you have been dismissed for absence but have obeyed all the rules regarding notification;
◆ failure to obey an instruction because of a misunderstanding;
◆ refusal to perform tasks because of a genuine religious or conscientious belief.

You should always be given a chance to comment on statements made against you by the provider or witnesses before a decision is made *(JSA 16/17, Ch 16, para 48)*.

It may be reasonable to **dismiss** you for natural clumsiness or inefficiency, for example, but it is not **misconduct**.

## JSA hardship provision

This is not the same as severe hardship provision. It is JSA paid at a reduced rate in certain circumstances to people in hardship. You can apply for payments under the JSA hardship provision if your JSA has been **stopped** or you are **waiting for a decision**.

In all the situations below, if you are claiming JSA as a member of a **prescribed group** (see page 28), you must show that **you or a member of your family would suffer hardship if hardship payments were not made**.

If you are claiming JSA on grounds of **severe hardship** and are waiting for a decision or have received a benefit penalty ((b)–(d) below), you are *entitled* to hardship payments. You do not have to prove you would otherwise suffer hardship as you have already proved severe hardship *(JSA 16/17, Ch 17, para 35)*. But you cannot get hardship payments if you have failed to fulfil labour market conditions ((a) below).

You can apply for hardship payments in the following circumstances *(JSA 16/17, Ch 17, para 19)*:

### a) JSA has been refused because you do not satisfy labour market conditions

You can claim hardship payments if JSA was refused because you are not available for work, not actively seeking employment and training, or will not complete and sign a Jobseeker's Agreement.

If you are claiming JSA on grounds of severe hardship, you cannot get hardship payments when you do not satisfy labour market conditions.

### b) You have been sanctioned

Most sanctions are for two weeks and include automatic entitlement to a reduced rate of JSA without the need to apply for hardship payments. But for some employment offences JSA is stopped (not reduced) for a period of 1–26 weeks. You get no payment unless you successfully claim hardship.

*c) You are waiting for a decision on whether you satisfy certain labour market conditions at the start of a claim and your JSA claim has not been processed*

These conditions are whether you are available for work, actively seeking employment and training, and have signed a Jobseeker's Agreement.

*d) Your JSA has been suspended until a decision is made on whether you satisfy certain labour market conditions.*

These conditions are whether you are available for work, actively seeking employment and training, and have signed a Jobseeker's Agreement.

The **amount of hardship provision** is your normal amount of JSA reduced by 40%, or reduced by 20% if you or a member of your family are pregnant or seriously ill *(AOG vol 6, para 40312)*.

If you are getting hardship payments you do not get credits of National Insurance contributions.

## How to claim

You will have to attend an interview at the Jobcentre and fill in an application form.

Jobcentre staff should not discourage you from applying for hardship payments *(JSA 16/17, Ch 17, para 47)*.

Awards of JSA hardship payments are usually paid two weeks in arrears. You can apply for a Social Fund payment to cover the time till the first payment is due (see Social Fund, page 64).

You will have to attend the Jobcentre for interview every two weeks before you get your payments.

## Summary of JSA sanctions

The rules about sanctions are extremely complicated. We summarise the main rules here, using our own codes for different sanctions. Look up the reason for a sanction in the table below, then check what the relevant sanction is in the list opposite.

| | Reason for sanction | Claimant group | Type of sanction |
|---|---|---|---|
| | Leaving employment voluntarily | prescribed | A |
| | | severe hardship | B |
| | Leaving employment because of misconduct | prescribed | A |
| | | severe hardship | B |
| | Refusing employment or neglecting to avail yourself of employment | prescribed | C |
| | | severe hardship | C |
| | Leaving training because of misconduct | prescribed | C |
| | | severe hardship | E |
| * | Leaving training early | prescribed | D |
| | | severe hardship | E |
| * | Refusing training | prescribed | D |
| | | severe hardship | E |
| | Failure to comply with a JS Direction | prescribed | F |
| | | severe hardship | G |

\*     New jobseekers should not be sanctioned for doing one of the starred items once.

**Sanction A:**
JSA stopped for 1-26 weeks. Decision made by SAO. You can appeal. You can apply for JSA hardship payments – you need to prove hardship.

**Sanction B:**
JSA stopped for 1-26 weeks. Decision made by SAO. You can appeal. You can apply for JSA hardship payments and do not have to prove hardship.

**Sanction C:**
JSA reduced for 2 weeks by 40%, or 20% if you or a member of your family is seriously ill or pregnant. Decision made by SAO. You can appeal.

**Sanction D:**
JSA reduced for 2 weeks by 40%, or 20% if you or a member of your family is seriously ill or pregnant. Decision made by LMAO. You can appeal.

**Sanction E:**
JSA reduced for 2 weeks (from start of next direction to pay JSA under severe hardship provision) by 40%, or 20% if you are seriously ill or pregnant. Decision made by ES Adviser on behalf of the Secretary of State. You cannot appeal.

**Sanction F:**
JSA stopped for 2 weeks. Decision made by SAO. You can appeal. You can apply for JSA hardship payments – you need to prove hardship.

**Sanction G:**
JSA stopped for 2 weeks. Decision made by SAO. You can appeal. You can apply for JSA hardship payments and do not have to prove hardship.

LMAO = Labour Market Adjudication Officer in local office/Jobcentre.
SAO = Sector Adjudication Officer in sector (regional) office.

*Source: JSA 16/17, Appendix 6, Labour Market Sanctions – Aide Memoire*

# OTHER BENEFITS

There are other benefits or loans that you may be able to get from the Benefits Agency. Benefits which are not means-tested, for example Severe Disablement Allowance, Maternity Allowance, Incapacity Benefit and Industrial Injuries Benefits, may be available to you. For more details see CPAG's *Rights Guide to Non-Means-Tested Benefits* (see page xviii).

## The Social Fund

You have no automatic right to any Social Fund payment from the discretionary part of the Social Fund scheme. Your case will be judged on its individual merits. Whether you get a payment will depend on how much money is available in your local office's fund, whether they think you can meet the repayments and how important they think your need is.

If you apply for a Social Fund payment and are refused, you have the right to ask for the decision to be reviewed, firstly in the local office, by the social fund officer, and then by the social fund inspector. If you are refused a payment you will be disqualified from applying again for the same reason for six months unless your circumstances change.

### Crisis loans

Crisis loans are available in an emergency or disaster to people over 16 who cannot get help from other sources, such as the local authority, family or friends, and if there is no other way of preventing serious risk to your own or your family's health and safety. You do not have to be on IS or JSA. If you are awarded one you will be expected to repay it in weekly instalments once the period of crisis is over.

Though loans are a burden as you have to pay them back, young people have used them to help them through short periods with no income, for example, for two weeks living expenses because JSA is paid in arrears. They are interest-free, so you pay back only what you borrow.

Normally crisis loans, like other social fund payments, are dealt with at the Benefits Agency office. However, in two situations you can apply for an crisis loan at the Jobcentre *(JSA 16/17, Ch 10, para 2)*:
✦ at the start of a claim where you are entitled to JSA or a hardship payment but the day for payment has not been reached; or
✦ where you have lost or not received your JSA giro, and a decision has been made not to replace the giro.

When you apply for a crisis loan in these circumstances the officer in the Jobcentre will telephone the Benefits Agency office and fax them a completed form. A decision will be made by a social fund officer at the Benefits Agency on the same day *(JSA 16/17, Ch 10, para 5)* and faxed to the Jobcentre.

If you disagree with the decision you can apply for a review in writing within 28 days.

If you have already applied for a loan and been turned down, but have since been told you will get JSA, you should reapply for a crisis loan.

### Budgeting loans
You can get a budgeting loan only if you have received IS/income-based JSA for six months without a break. Loans likely to be given highest priority are for items such as essential household furniture or bedding, where, if you did not receive the money, your health or safety might be at risk. Money cannot be lent for deposits to pay to a landlord letting a flat or a house.

### Community care grants
Community care grants do not have to be repaid. They are to help people who have been living in places like hospitals, hostels for

homeless people and detention centres, or people who are moving out of local authority care into other housing.

Community care grants are available only to people who are on IS/JSA or who will be leaving institutional or residential care (e.g. local authority care, prison, hospital, hostels, supported lodgings) within six weeks and are likely to get IS/JSA on discharge.

## Housing Benefit

There are no special rules which disentitle 16/17 year olds from Housing Benefit. Unemployed 16/17 year olds who are living independently and have responsibility for paying rent are eligible. Young people who have been refused JSA or are on YTBA can claim Housing Benefit. Young people have sometimes been refused Housing Benefit on the basis that they have no income – this should not be done. Young people who live with parents or a brother or a sister cannot claim Housing Benefit. You need to be paying rent on a commercial basis.

You should claim Housing Benefit from your local authority.

For detailed advice on young people and housing, consult the benefits guides published by CHAR – The Housing Campaign for Single People, 5-15 Cromer Street, London WC1H 8LS; phone: 0171 833 2071.

## Severe Disablement Allowance (SDA)

SDA is a weekly cash benefit for people who have been incapable of work for at least 28 weeks but who do not have enough National Insurance contributions to qualify for Incapacity Benefit.

16 and 17 year olds who receive SDA and who also claim IS will be paid IS at the higher rate together with the disability premium. This means their IS entitlement may exceed their SDA and they will be paid the difference as IS.

# HABITUAL RESIDENCE TEST

The Habitual Residence Test was introduced in August 1994. It is a condition of entitlement for people claiming JSA, IS, Housing Benefit and Council Tax Benefit. Anyone considered to be 'not habitually resident' in the UK, Republic of Ireland, Channel Islands and Isle of Man may be classed as a 'person from abroad' and refused benefit. Any new or repeat claimant since August 1994 who appears to have come to live in this country within the last five years may be called in for interview.

The interview looks at such matters as:·
✦ where is your 'centre of interest' – where have you spent most of your life, where your possessions are, whether you are a member of any clubs or societies in the UK, whether you are registered for YT or on a YT scheme, where the members of your family who give you most support are;
✦ where you have been employed in the past, and the type of occupation;
✦ when you came to the UK: the longer you have been here, the stronger your case might be;
✦ where else you have lived and for how long;
✦ where your family is;
✦ what your intentions are.

There is no time limit before or after which you are definitely 'habitually resident' or not. You are likely to have problems with the Habitual Residence Test if you have been in the country for less than five years.

You can appeal to an independent tribunal. It may take 3-6 months before your appeal is heard. It may well be worth appealing as many appeals have been successful, especially with representation. Good advice and representation is important.

Get advice on how to survive while waiting for your appeal to be heard. It might be possible to try for a severe hardship payment. You will probably need very good advice and representation for this.

You can get more information from the handbook published by the Joint Council for the Welfare of Immigrants, 115 Old St, London EC1V 9JZ, and from CPAG's *National Welfare Benefits Handbook* (see page xviii).

If you are an asylum seeker you can get advice from the Refugee Council, Bondway House, 3/9 Bondway, London SW8 1SJ. They have lists of local refugee groups.

If you are a refugee or want to become a refugee, you should get advice because it has become much harder to get benefit since changes in February 1996.

## PART TWO
# TRAINING PROGRAMMES

As explained in Part One of this Guide, most 16 and 17 year olds are not entitled to Income Support or Jobseeker's Allowance. Instead they are 'guaranteed' a training place. Since 1990, Youth Training has been the main training scheme for this age group. More recently, Modern Apprenticeships have been added. There are plans to introduce National Traineeships and Relaunch in September 1997.

This part of the Guide describes these schemes: their aims, the eligibility rules, the requirements on TECs/LECs to give you support, your terms and conditions while on a scheme and the payments you may receive. It also describes the complex rules of the Guarantee.

The aims of TEC funding for young people are *(TEC PP, para C1):*

> "to provide young people, through work experience, key skills and fostering individual commitment to lifelong learning, with the breadth and flexibility of skill that industry, commerce and the economy needs in its future workforce and to secure greater co-operation in planning FE College provision which is more responsive to employers'/labour market needs and priorities for growth."

Youth Training and Modern Apprenticeships are delivered through Youth Credits, which have a variety of local names. Young people are given a Youth Credit with which they can 'buy' training. In Scotland, YT is now only residual and has been superseded by the introduction of Skillseekers. Modern Apprenticeships for 16 and 17 year olds are also accessed and funded through Skillseekers in Scotland.

The first section of this part of the Guide describes how the Youth Credits scheme is intended to work and the situations you may actually be in if you hold a Youth Credit.

# YOUTH CREDITS

## What are Youth Credits?

A Youth Credit represents an entitlement to train to approved standards for 16 and 17 year olds leaving full-time education. Each credit has a financial value and can be used by a young person to obtain training with an employer or training provider. Youth Credits were known nationally as Training Credits until April 1993.

Youth Credits are the way young people access YT and Modern Apprenticeships. They are operated locally through TECs and LECs.

They have different names in different areas. In London they are called 'Network'. Several areas are using the term 'Training Credits'. Examples of other names are 'Careerships' (South and East Cheshire), 'Prospects' (Gwent) and 'Future' (Merseyside). In Scotland the programme is called 'Skillseekers'.

Training delivered under Youth Credits is subject to the conditions and rules set out in the TEC/LEC contract explained in the section on YT.

Within the general guidelines for Youth Credits given to TECs and LECs, individual areas have developed schemes in their own way. This has led to wide variations between areas. In explaining how Youth Credits work we give the national rules which apply to all areas and some examples of the variations between areas.

# Aims of Youth Credits

Youth Credits should *(AFA, para B1.1)*:

✦ encourage and motivate more young people leaving full-time education at age 16 or 17 to enter training and secure more and higher levels of skills and qualifications;

✦ encourage and support the development of improved local careers and guidance services for young people;

✦ help create more efficient and responsive local markets in training;

✦ increase flexibility, strengthen existing training arrangements and encourage more employers to provide training for young people; and thereby improve individual choice.

# Who runs Youth Credits?

Youth Credits are mostly paid for by the Government. The administration of Youth Credits in England is the responsibility of the DfEE, in Wales of the Welsh Office and in Scotland of Scottish Enterprise and Highlands & Islands Enterprise.

At a local level TECs or LECs are responsible for day-to-day delivery and they decide whether to contract out the organisation of the training or organise it themselves. In practice three models have emerged:

✦ agent-based schemes building on the existing YT infrastructure of providers (see page 80);

✦ employer-based schemes in which the TEC/LEC mainly contracts with employers;

✦ schemes in which the TEC/LEC carries out the agent role itself and contracts with others for specific services.

# Information about Youth Credits

General information about credits in England is available from the DfEE, but the TEC/LEC in each area is responsible for making its own arrangements for publicity – e.g. posters, videos, leaflets and freephone helplines.

TECs must ensure that all young people in the final year of compulsory education are informed of their entitlement to a Youth Credit and are advised on how to obtain and use one *(TEC PP, para C18.2)*.

# The issue of credits

Most TEC/LECs arrange for the Careers Service to issue the credits on their behalf.

The decision about the process for issuing the credits is made locally by the TEC/LEC. As a result, the timing and number of credits issued varies between areas. In some areas, for example, credits are issued to all 16 and 17 year olds, even those continuing in full-time education. In others they are issued to young people only when they express an intention of leaving full-time education in the immediate future.

The physical appearance of the credit which a young person receives varies from area to area. It could, for example, be a 'passport', a 'credit card', a 'smart card' or a 'cheque book'.

# Value of the credit

Many credits show a monetary face value: this is often done by showing a minimum, average or notional value which credit holders may realise.

Some areas have a basic rate with supplements, for example, for skill shortage occupations and special training needs. Other schemes have a banding system with, for example, occupational categories, NVQ/SVQ level or size of employer determining the value. So the value of the credit will vary depending on where you live, the skill area you are training in and so on.

If the value of the credit does not cover your training costs the TEC or employer should top it up:

> "There will be no question of the person receiving the training being asked to top it up from his or her own resources."
> *(Michael Howard, Hansard, 27/3/90, col. 212)*

# Preparing for and using the credit

## Situations of Youth Credit holders

A person under 18 years old who leaves full-time education will fall into one of the following categories:

### *(a) Using the credit in work time*

If you are in a job, you may follow a training programme using your credit.

### *(b) Own-time trainees*

If you are in work but are unable to use the training credit with your employer, you may enrol for training in your own time and use your credit to pay for your training.

### *(c) In work and not using the credit*

You may be in full-time employment but not using your credit as you or your employer is not aware of the entitlement to a credit or does not wish to participate in training.

### (d) Non-employed, in full-time training and receiving an allowance

You may be unable to find a job and instead go on a training scheme. In this case you use your credit for the training, which is usually arranged for you by whoever is running the training scheme. Your training provider should pay you at least the minimum training allowance.

### (e) Unemployed young people

Despite the YT guarantees some young people are without a job or a training place. If at any time you have no money because a suitable training place has not been found, you may be eligible for the YT Bridging Allowance or JSA or your parents may be eligible for Child Benefit. If none of these are available or they would not provide you with enough money to live on you have a right to make a claim for JSA under the severe hardship rules (see Part One for more details about benefits).

As outlined above, the situations of credit holders can vary widely. The rest of this section outlines the process that should be followed to enable you to make the best use of your credit.

## Enhanced guidance and Individual Action Plans

You are entitled to comprehensive careers education and guidance from your local careers service, including information about credits. Your careers guidance should result in an Individual Action Plan. An Individual Action Plan outlines your career goals and the steps which need to be taken to achieve those goals. It is usually drawn up by you with the help of a careers officer.

## Individual Training Plan (ITP)

When you start using your credit or within a week of starting training you should be given an ITP that you have agreed *(TEC PP, para C32.1)*. (See page 89.)

## Activating the credit

When the ITP has been drawn up and approved, the credit is 'activated'. The TEC/LEC can then start to release the money allocated to it.

Varying amounts of the credit allocated to an individual are released at different stages during the period of entitlement. Individual TECs/LECs have local variations, but payments are often linked either to specific achievements, such as gaining qualifications, or to particular stages of the training, such as the number of training weeks delivered.

The training provider will claim funding from the TEC/LEC at appropriate points and the young person may have to endorse the payment to be debited from his/her credit.

Depending on the form of the credit, the way the endorsement occurs will vary between areas. For example, young people may sign a 'cheque', or be allocated a PIN number for their 'smart card' which they will then use in the 'swipe' machine.

## Who holds the credit?

In theory you should hold your credit, but in practice many training providers hold the credits themselves, requiring you to sign them in advance or giving you access only when you need to sign to release the payment. This runs counter to the idea that Youth Credits give you more control over your training.

The credit is yours. If your training provider wants to keep it for you, but you are not happy about this, you can consult your careers officer or TEC/LEC.

## Losing your credit

If you lose your credit, you should be able to get a replacement from the TEC/LEC. Again this is usually via the Careers Service. If some of the credit has already been used, the TEC/LEC should have a record of this and of the amount still credited to you.

## Time limits for using the credit

Time limits for using the credit vary between areas. In some areas young people may have to use their allocated credit within three years; in other areas it may be longer. Check with your TEC/LEC. You cannot stay on Modern Apprenticeships or YT past your 25th birthday *(TEC PP, para C19.2)*.

## Changes while on a Youth Credits scheme

### *Changing training provider*
Once the value of the credit has been allocated, that amount of credit remains allocated to you to continue the same training. If you change to another approved training provider in the same TEC/LEC area, the balance of the credit normally goes with you. Check with your TEC/LEC.

### *Changing course*
You are usually given a chance to change your mind about your chosen area of skill training. However, the rules set down by your TEC/LEC determine whether you lose some of your credit entitlement and if so, how much. In some areas the value of your credit may be 'topped up' to its original value if you change course within a given period, for

example within the first three months. In other areas any time already spent in training is deducted from your entitlement.

*Moving out of the area*

If a young person moves to another TEC/LEC area the responsibility for the training normally moves to the new area of residence. However, the individual TEC/LEC which issued the original Youth Credit may continue to fund the young person's training, as there are no rules to prevent this. As a result there are no clear guidelines that can be given for an individual in this situation other than the TEC/LEC obligations to meet the YT Guarantee (see page 82).

Different TEC/LEC areas give different overall entitlement: who is eligible, length of time for completion of training and entitlement if you change course may all vary. Check with your TEC/LEC.

## Rights on Youth Credits

If you are using your Youth Credit to access YT or Modern Apprentice-ships, then all rights, terms and conditions, training allowance rates, benefits and other payments are those for the relevant scheme as described in the following sections.

## Special training needs

TECs/LECs have to ensure that 'Suitable high quality and individually tailored Training shall be available to Trainees who have a Disability or Special Training Needs.' *(TEC PP, para C29.2)*.

If you have a special training need or disability your TEC or LEC may ensure:

✦ that you receive extra guidance on how you might use your credit;
✦ that your credit is valid for a longer period of training.

# YOUTH TRAINING

## What is Youth Training?

Youth Training (YT) is the primary training scheme for unemployed young people. It is accessed through Youth Credits. YT replaced YTS in May 1990. In Scotland most YT has been replaced by Skillseekers.

## Aims of YT

The stated aims of YT are *(AFA, para B5.1):*

+ to help eligible young people to acquire the **broadly-based training** required for a flexible, self-reliant and productive workforce;
+ to provide training for eligible people which, dependent on their abilities, leads to an Approved Qualification at or above National Vocational Qualification (NVQ) or Scottish Vocational Qualification (SVQ) level 2 standard;
+ to meet the skill needs of the economy.

---

**Broadly-based training** is defined as training which, in addition to the competencies required for an approved qualification, includes basic literacy and numeracy, computer awareness, enterprising behaviour and the ability to adapt and transfer skills between different working contexts or different occupations.

---

# Who runs YT?

YT is mostly paid for by the Government. The DfEE is responsible for its administration in England. The Welsh Office is responsible for the administration of YT in Wales and the Scottish Office in Scotland. In Scotland the Scottish Office delegates this responsibility to Scottish Enterprise and Highlands & Islands Enterprise (see page 6).

YT is operated locally through TECs and LECs (see page 5). To retain their licences, TECs and LECs must meet the Youth Guarantee *(TEC Standards (draft), para A2.3)*, that is ensure that young people in the YT Guarantee Groups are offered training opportunities as outlined in this chapter.

TECs/LECs may organise the training themselves, but more commonly contract with YT providers to run the training programmes. YT providers may be local authorities, chambers of commerce, voluntary organisations, colleges of further education, private employers, industrial training groups or private training providers.

YT providers are responsible, for example, for making sure you get proper training, paying your allowance and ensuring that where you train is safe and that you are not prevented from benefiting from YT because of your race, religion, sex or disability.

Sub-contractors can be used by YT providers to provide all or part of the training programme. Sub-contractors may be other employers or organisations, e.g. a local college may be sub-contracted to provide off-the-job training. The sub-contractor must offer you the same minimum terms and conditions as your YT provider.

# Recruitment to YT

YT providers can use any method they want to recruit and select young people for the YT training programmes they run.

Most trainees are recruited through the Careers Service. The Careers Service may be run by the local education authority, the TEC/LEC, a private contractor or any mixture of these. It is its job to offer help and advice to young people looking for jobs, training or further education. The Careers Service is given some funds by the Government for its role in referring young people to YT.

If you want to join YT, the Careers Service should know about the YT places available in your area and about places elsewhere if you want to train in an occupation for which there is no training available locally.

# Who can go on YT?

In relation to YT, you fall into one of four groups:
+ not eligible;
+ not guaranteed, but eligible;
+ in the Guarantee Group (as a 'first time entrant' or 'returner', see below);
+ in the extended Guarantee Group.

## Eligibility

Most young people are eligible to join YT. However, the number of places for young people outside the Guarantee Group is limited by the funds available in each area.

You are eligible for YT or Modern Apprenticeships if you *(TEC PP, para C19)*:

✦ have reached the minimum school leaving age and are under 25 years old;

✦ are not attending school or college as a full-time pupil or student;

✦ are not in higher education;

✦ are not an overseas national subject to employment or training restrictions and/or to a time limit on your stay in Great Britain (other than a refugee or an asylum seeker);

✦ are not taking part in any other employment, training or enterprise programme or scheme funded by the Secretaries of State;

✦ are not in custody as a prisoner or on remand in custody.

# The YT Guarantee

Most unemployed 16 and 17 year olds cannot get IS or JSA. Instead the Government guarantees a place on YT. This means that if you are unemployed, YT may be the only way you can get an income. (See Part One for other income that unemployed young people may be able to get.)

The Youth Training Guarantee Group covers all young people who satisfy the above eligibility criteria and *(TEC PP, C: Words and Expressions)*:

✦ are not employed or self-employed; and

✦ are seeking entry into YT; and

✦ are not in full-time education; and

✦ have not reached the age of 18 (but see the extended Guarantee, page 86).

## Place of residence

The geographical or 'operational' area that a TEC covers is defined in its Corporate Plan (see page 8). You are defined as being resident in the TEC's area if, when eligibility is determined, you declare that you reside in the TEC's area. Residence is not dependent upon having a fixed address *(TEC PP, C: Words and Expressions)*. Your word should be accepted on this matter.

You should not be refused access to YT if you are eligible for YT but not resident in the TEC operational area *(TEC PP, para C30.1)*.

## Support

In order to ensure that you have access to youth training, the TEC has responsibilities to provide support to residents in the Guarantee Groups. For more details see page 113.

# Offers of places on YT under the Guarantee

## The offer of a training opportunity

A 'training opportunity' is defined as an opportunity offered to you to engage in and to complete suitable full-time training specified in an Individual Training Plan. It can be part-time if the TEC's contract permits it and you agree *(TEC PP, C: Words and Expressions)*.

A training opportunity is judged to be suitable if it is vocationally relevant in certain respects, namely *(TEC PP, C: Words and Expressions)*:
+ personal capacity;
+ aptitude;
+ trainee's preference;
+ employer's preference;
+ level of approved qualification aimed at;
+ duration of training;
+ proximity;
+ prompt availability.

An 'offer' of a training opportunity is defined as an offer made by a training provider or an offer made by a Careers Office to attend an interview for a training opportunity with a provider which you refuse or fail to attend without good cause *(TEC PP, C: Words and Expressions)*.

If you have a good cause (see page 54) to reject a training opportunity it is not counted as an offer made to you *(TEC PP, para C24)*.

## First time entrants

You are a 'first time entrant' if *(TEC PP, C: Words and Expressions)*:
◆ you are a member of the YT Guarantee Group;
◆ you are a resident in the TEC's area;
◆ you have not been employed (including self-employed) for 16 or more hours a week; and
◆ you register with the Careers Service as seeking first time entry to YT.

As a first time entrant you are entitled to assessment and up to two offers (the second if you reject the first) of a training opportunity.

In England and Wales you will fall into one of the following categories depending on when you leave school *(TEC PP, para C21.1)*:

(a) If you leave full-time education before Easter 1997, then the offer or offers shall be to start within eight weeks from your registering with the Careers Service.

(b) If you leave full-time education between Easter 1997 and 22 May 1997 inclusive then the offer or offers shall be to start by 1 July 1997 or eight weeks from your registering with the Careers Service, whichever is later.

(c) If you leave full-time education on or after 23 May 1997 and before Easter 1998 then the offer shall be to start by 2 January 1998 or eight weeks from your registering with the Careers Service, whichever is later.

The Guarantee in Scotland takes account of different school leaving dates.

If, as a first time entrant, you reject a training opportunity 'without good cause' you should be offered a second training opportunity which starts within the time limits set out in (a) to (c) above (whichever is appropriate). If you have not taken up training after two suitable offers, the TEC only has to offer you further training opportunities as if you were a 'returner' (see below).

*18 years old and a first time entrant*
If you are a first time entrant and reach the age of 18 before being made an offer, you are entitled to assessment and **one** offer of a training opportunity to start as in (a) to (c) above *(TEC PP, para C21.1)*.

## Returners

You are a 'returner' if you are a member of the YT Guarantee Group who is a resident (see page 83) and has registered or re-registered and who since first leaving full-time education *(TEC PP, C: Words and Expressions)*:

✦ has been employed (including self-employed) for 16 or more hours a week; or

✦ has completed a YT training course or a Modern Apprenticeship; or

✦ has attended a YT training course or a Modern Apprenticeship but your course has prematurely terminated; or

✦ has rejected without good cause offers of training opportunities made to you as a first time entrant (see above).

You should be offered assessment or reassessment and an offer of one training opportunity to start within eight weeks ('the initial period') of registering or re-registering with the Careers Service as seeking YT training.

If you reject the training opportunity without good cause (see definition page 54) but continue to be a member of the YT Guarantee Group you can re-register with the Careers Service and request a further training opportunity to start within eight weeks of either *(TEC PP, para C22.1)*:

✦ the initial period; or

✦ your re-registering with the Careers Service as seeking YT; whichever is later.

You can continue to re-register with the Careers Service to be offered further training opportunities, but the TEC/LEC has to offer only one training opportunity per eight-week period until you cease to be a member of the Guarantee Group.

*18 years old and a returner*

If your 18th birthday falls in one of these eight-week periods, you are entitled to one final offer of a training opportunity *(TEC PP, para C22.2)*.

## The YT extended Guarantee Group

You are a member of the YT extended Guarantee Group if you satisfy the YT eligibility criteria (see page 82), are non-employed and seeking entry into YT, and *(TEC PP, C: Words and Expressions)*:

✦ have reached the age of 18 but have not been available to enter training for the first time because of:
  – disability,
  – ill health,
  – pregnancy,
  – custodial sentence,
  – remand in custody,
  – language difficulties, or
  – as a result of a care order; or

✦ entered training for the first time before reaching the age of 18 but discontinued your training for any of the reasons set out in the above list and were unable to resume your training before reaching the age of 18.

If you are a member of the YT extended Guarantee Group the TEC has to provide you with assessment and a single training opportunity which starts within eight weeks of your registering with the Careers Service as seeking YT *(TEC PP, para C23.1)*.

## Young people with disabilities

You are seen as having a disability if you have "a physical or mental impairment which has a substantial and long term adverse effect on [your] ability to carry out normal day to day activities". This is the definition used in the Disability Discrimination Act 1995 *(TEC PP, C: Words and Expressions)*.

The TEC must ensure that you receive adequate support *(TEC PP, para C30.2)*. 'Support' means help to enable you to take up and continue in training such as aids and adaptations or fares *(TEC PP, C: Words and Expressions)*. For more details see page 114.

If you are over 18 but were not available for YT when you were under 18 because of a disability, then you are guaranteed the offer (but not the re-offer) of a suitable place on YT. You have to have finished your YT training by your 25th birthday.

You should not be discriminated against because of any disability you may have (see 'Equal opportunities' below, page 97).

You may be entitled to disability benefits (see page 117).

## Previous definitions of the Guarantee Group

If you are already in training or on a Modern Apprenticeship, your entitlement to complete it will not be prejudiced by any changes in the eligibility criteria *(TEC PP, para C19.3)*.

## Preparatory Training and the Guarantee

If a training course cannot start within the time limits outlined above, members of the YT Guarantee Group and the YT extended Guarantee Group will be given Preparatory Training (see page 91) to start within the same time limits. This should lead to training to NVQ standard which will start within eight weeks of the end of Preparatory Training *(TEC PP, para C25)*.

## If the Guarantee is not met

Although the Careers Service usually looks for training places for young people, it is ultimately the TEC/LEC that 'shall meet' the YT guarantee *(TEC PP, para C20.1)*. Those in the Guarantee Groups must have priority in the offer of places over all other eligible young people *(TEC PP, para C20.1)*.

The TEC must 'record and investigate' complaints that the Guarantee is not being met. If the complaint is valid the TEC must remedy it. If a remedy is not achievable the TEC must notify the Secretary of State in writing *(TEC PP, para C28.2)*. A LEC must report to Scottish Enterprise or Highlands & Islands Enterprise.

If you are in difficulty because a suitable YT place has not been found, you can contact the TEC/LEC and ask for the guarantee liaison officer or an appropriate person. The TEC/LEC should investigate any problems in meeting the Guarantee and find a place for you as soon as possible. You should be kept informed of progress.

If at any time you have no money because a suitable YT place has not been found, you may be eligible for Bridging Allowance or JSA or your parents may be eligible for Child Benefit (see Part One). If none of these are available or they would not provide you with enough money to live on you have a right to make a claim for JSA under severe hardship rules.

## After achieving an NVQ level 2

Unless you are endorsed as having category A or B Special Training Needs (see page 93), your training should enable you to achieve at least one approved qualification at or above NVQ/SVQ level 2 standard. If you get such a qualification, as specified in your Individual Training Plan (ITP) or Apprenticeship Plan, and would otherwise enter the YT Guarantee Group on leaving, you may remain in training and be offered an extended or new ITP/Apprenticeship Plan. In such a case there is no requirement for the ITP to specify an approved qualification at or above NVQ/SVQ level 2 standard.

# Assessment of training needs

The TEC has to ensure that you are assessed before or immediately on entry into training *(TEC PP, para C29.1)*.

Assessment is defined as 'an initial diagnosis of guidance need, access to careers and labour market information and other guidance activity that is structured, confidential, impartial and individually tailored'. The outcomes should be *(TEC PP, C: Words and Expressions)*:

✦ increased understanding of yourself, your needs and what you want to achieve;
✦ increased knowledge of the realistic options available;
✦ increased ability to make realistic occupational decisions;
✦ increased ability to plan action to implement decisions.

## Individual Training Plans

When you start YT, or within one week of entry, you should be given an ITP that you have agreed with your training provider *(TEC PP, para C32.1)*. Your ITP must be such that you have a reasonable prospect of completing it successfully. It should also specify a reasonable duration of training in view of your training needs and the nature and level of qualifications you are aiming for *(TEC PP, para C32.2.1)*.

The ITP has to be kept up to date and be amended to reflect any variation in content agreed by you and your training provider.

The ITP should include *(TEC PP, para C32.2)*:

✦ your prior learning and assessed training needs;

✦ your name and signature;

✦ a statement that training is to be carried out under YT rules and requirements or a local, written set of arrangements which offer you at least as much as the YT rules – you must be able to see these written arrangements;

✦ the start date for training and the intended leaving date;

✦ your weekly hours of attendance;

✦ any agreed trainee support arrangements (see page 113);

✦ the name, level and reference number of at least one whole approved qualification which you aim to achieve. Unless you have been endorsed as having Category A or B special training needs (see page 93), that approved qualification must be at NVQ level 2 or higher standard;

✦ a brief statement of your employment or career objectives.

Any changes to the plans must be agreed with you *(TEC PP, para C34.1)*.


*Dissatisfaction with ITPs*

If you express reasonable dissatisfaction with the delivery of your ITP or, in the opinion of the TEC or your training provider, you are no longer making satisfactory progress on your ITP, you should be offered alternative training with the TEC or the same provider or another provider on the basis of a new ITP *(TEC PP, para C34.2)*.

Any change to your existing training course or any transfer to another training provider has to be subject to your consent. However if your consent is 'unreasonably withheld' you may be required to discontinue your training *(TEC PP, para C34.2)*.

If the provider can no longer provide training to you in accordance with your ITP, e.g. the provider closed down the scheme, the TEC has to ensure that you are offered the opportunity to transfer, with a substantially similar ITP, to another provider *(TEC PP, para C34.3)*.

## Training records

You should be given a National Record of Achievement (NRA) when you start your YT if you do not already have one. Your NRA should be kept up to date.

## Preparatory Training

Preparatory Training is 'training for people, unable to enter Training, which is intended to facilitate subsequent entry into a vocational course within Youth Training' *(TEC PP, C: Words and Expressions)*. It may be offered to you before you start YT.

Preparatory Training is designed for people whose entry into a mainstream YT course is debarred because of:
✦ low motivation; or
✦ need for prior assessment; or
✦ lack of clear vocational preference; or
✦ lack of initial language or other skills essential for entry into a vocational course.

You may be referred to Preparatory Training if you are guaranteed a YT place, but a suitable one is not available (see page 88). In some areas arrangements have been made between hostels and Preparatory Training schemes which allow young people to receive an allowance, take part in training and look for accommodation.

While on Preparatory Training you should be paid at least the minimum training allowance and your terms and conditions are the same as if you were on YT.

If you are in a Guarantee Group, you must be offered a mainstream YT place offering training to NVQ standard to start within eight weeks of completing Preparatory Training *(TEC PP, para C25)*.

## Special training needs

TECs and LECs have to ensure that *(TEC PP, para C29.2)*:

> "Suitable high quality and individually tailored Training shall be available to a Trainee who has a Disability or Special Training Needs."

Special training needs are defined as *(TEC PP, C: Words and Expressions)*:

> "The training needs arising from any personal disadvantage which significantly impairs your ability to undergo successfully a course of Training or Apprenticeship."

This could include literacy and numeracy difficulties, physical or sensory impairment, mental illness, learning difficulties, chronic ill health, emotional and behavioural problems, difficult personal circumstances, problems associated with prolonged absence from work, problems associated with drug/solvent/alcohol abuse and difficulties with English because it is not your first language *(TEC STN)*.

TECs must include a description of the provision for young people with special training needs and any special arrangements with providers planned to meet these needs in their Business Plans *(TEC PP, para C3.3)*.

In Scotland you have special training needs if, at the time of assessment, you have no reasonable prospects of achieving a qualification at SVQ level 2 or equivalent.

## Identification of special training needs

The TEC has to ensure that all young people resident in its area who are eligible for YT or already on YT and have a special training need are properly identified.

The Careers Service (or identifying organisation) must supply an endorsement certificate for you if you are identified as having a special training need. The certificate is given to your YT provider when you enter training. It should be based on objective tests and an examination of the available evidence *(TEC PP, C: Words and Expressions)*.

YT providers can refer back anyone they consider as incorrectly identified, including those who appear to have special training needs which have not been recognised.

The certificate must state that your special training need falls into one of the following three categories *(TEC PP, para C29.3)*:

Category A    you require Preparatory Training before you join mainstream YT;

Category B    you have no realistic prospect of achieving an approved qualification at NVQ level 2 standard;

Category C    you might be able to get an approved qualification at NVQ level 2 if you had significant additional support and help.

If appropriate you may also be endorsed as belonging to *(TEC PP, para C29.4)*:

Category L    you need foundation level literacy training, including English for Speakers of Other Languages; and/or

Category N    you need foundation level numeracy training.

You will be given training up to foundation level Wordpower or Numberpower standard.

In Scotland the following categories are used instead:

✦ you are following a VQ level 2 or above and require additional funding to pay for additional support to enable your special training needs to be met;

✦ you are following a VQ level 1;

✦ you are following a training programme below VQ level 1.

## *Special training needs and the Guarantees*

If you are endorsed as Category A and go onto Preparatory Training as a member of the Guarantee Group or the extended Guarantee Group and you finish your Preparatory Training or are ready to enter a vocational course of YT before finishing Preparatory Training, you should be treated as if entering YT for the first time under the YT Guarantee or the YT extended Guarantee, so points (a) to (c) on page 84 apply to you.

## Leaving YT

On leaving YT you should immediately be given written notice of termination *(TEC PP, para C31.5)*.

Your YT provider cannot ask you for compensation if you are a non-employed trainee and you leave the scheme before the leaving date stipulated in your ITP.

You can leave YT any time you want to. However, if you do not have a job to go to you may find yourself in financial difficulties. Most people under 18 are not entitled to JSA – though every 16/17 year old has the right to apply for JSA under the severe hardship provisions. You may be entitled to Bridging Allowance if you reapply for a YT place. (For details of what unemployed under 18s are entitled to see Part One.)

People over and under 18 who want to claim JSA may find, depending on the circumstances under which they left YT, that their benefit could be cut or disallowed. Consideration will be given to whether you had 'good cause' for leaving *(JSA Regs, reg 73)* (see page 54).

If you left YT because the training was substandard, the AO should ask whether you tried to get this put right, and if so how. If you produce a letter from the Careers Service confirming that you made a complaint which could be supported, the AO should accept that you had good cause. If you followed the grievance procedure and complained to the YT provider, the DSS will check with the YT provider.

The AO should take into account *(AOG, vol 6, paras 39797–9):*
+ your age and experience;
+ the fact that young people may not understand complaints procedures and may be too frightened to ask anyone other than their immediate supervisor.

But if you made no attempt to use the grievance procedure you will usually be unable to show good cause.

If you state that the Careers Service advised you to leave, they will be asked for confirmation and the reasons for their advice. If the AO is still in doubt s/he will ask the TEC/LEC:
+ if their monitoring of the scheme involved is up to date;
+ whether they consider your allegations well founded.

Good cause should be accepted if *(AOG, vol 6, para 39800):*
+ the agreed training programme was not being followed;
+ you tried to resolve the problem by a reasonable approach to:
    – the YT provider involved, or
    – the Careers Service, or
    – the TEC/LEC, or
    – the ES District Manager or local Jobcentre.

## Transferring from YT to TfW, JIG and Jobclubs

Time spent on YT counts as a break in unemployment. Applicants for Training for Work (TfW) or the Job Interview Guarantee (JIG) who have been on YT will need to have been unemployed for at least 26 weeks to qualify for entry to TfW or JIG via the main route. However you can enter TfW or JIG immediately if you are eligible to do so via the exception groups, for example you have a disability or you need foundation level literacy and/or numeracy training.

YT leavers who are over 18 can join a Jobclub immediately. (The *Unemployment and Training Rights Handbook* gives more details – see page 149).

# Your rights on YT: terms and conditions

## Non-employed or employed trainee

On YT you are either a non-employed trainee or an employed trainee or, in a few cases, self-employed. At all times you must be clearly identified as one of these *(TEC PP, para C31.1)*.

You must be notified in writing of the terms and conditions of your training when you start *(TEC PP, para C31.1)*. You must also be notified in writing of any subsequent changes.

As a non-employed trainee you have limited legal rights at work, but you are entitled to certain national terms and conditions set out in the TEC or LEC contract. However there are specific areas in which the TECs and LECs have the flexibility to determine local conditions.

The TEC's definition of authorised absence must be set out in the Business Plan *(TEC PP, para C3.9)*. In Scotland LECs must agree definitions with Scottish Enterprise/Highlands & Islands Enterprise. These definitions should cover:
✦ authorised sickness absence;
✦ other authorised absence from training (see page 102);
✦ paid holidays.

The TEC or LEC has the power to determine conditions for trainees in respect of:

✦ grievance and disciplinary procedures;

✦ trade union membership;

✦ parental permission for YT trainees under 18, e.g. for participation in residential work or working unusual hours.

If you are an employed trainee you are in the same position in relation to the law as any other employed young person. How good your terms and conditions are will depend on what you are offered in your contract of employment. Though you are in a job which should continue when your training ends, you will not necessarily have better terms and conditions than a non-employed trainee on all matters.

## Equal opportunities

The TEC must ensure that its providers and their contractors agree to promote equal opportunities for all activities funded under the Secretaries of State.

It must have a strategy for equal opportunities, including *(TEC Standards (draft), para C4.1)*:

✦ a statement of its overall objective for securing equality of opportunity across all its activities;

✦ an assessment of current performance;

✦ plans for eliminating shortfalls;

✦ a statement of local community groups consulted; and

✦ a commitment to publish a statement in its Annual Report.

There are specific laws covering sex discrimination, racial discrimination, and discrimination on the grounds of disability. If your YT provider or a sub-contractor discriminates against you because of your sex, race, religion or disability in offering access to training or terminating training, they are breaking the law. You have the right to take your case to industrial tribunal *(SD Act 75, sec 14; RR Act 76, sec 13 Disability Act 95)*.

The provisions of the Disability Discrimination Act are outlined in *A brief guide to the Disability Discrimination Act* available from Disability on the Agenda, FREEPOST, Bristol BS38 7DE, or telephone 0345 622 633.

You should not be discriminated against because you have been punished for breaking the law or because you are a lesbian or a gay man.

Harassment (like name-calling, physical threats or violence) because of your race, religion, sex, disability or sexual orientation should not be acceptable on your scheme. Whether it is staff, other trainees or you who is responsible for the harassment, it should be treated as a disciplinary matter and could result in disciplinary action.

### If you are discriminated against

If you are discriminated against you should follow your scheme's grievance procedure (see page 104).

The TEC has to 'ensure that any allegations of discrimination made against it are properly investigated and appropriate action taken'. If any cases are referred to an industrial tribunal the TEC has to notify the relevant Secretary of State immediately. Details of any such complaints and allegations and how they were resolved must be included in the TEC's Annual Report *(TEC Standards (draft), para C4.2)*.

If you think your YT provider might have broken the law, the following offer more specialised help:

The Commission for Racial Equality. The Headquarters are at Elliot House, 10/12 Allington Street, London SW1E 5EH (phone: 0171 828 7022).

The Equal Opportunities Commission, Overseas House, Quay Street, Manchester M3 3HN (phone: 0161 833 92440) – particularly for advice on the Sex Discrimination Act.

If you are disabled and your employer has discriminated against you, you can ask ACAS (the Advisory Conciliation and Arbitration Service) or in Northern Ireland the LRA (Labour Relations Agency) to help you.

## Hours

*All trainees*

The hours you are asked to work must comply with national legislation and any appropriate local by-laws. For instance shop assistants are entitled to meal breaks and to a weekly half-day off. For more details contact your Health and Safety Executive area office (see the phone book or ask in your local library).

Most of the specific controls on the hours that young people can work including shift work, night work and length of hours were removed with the 1989 Employment Act. But you should not have to work excessive hours or unsuitable shift patterns likely to lead to ill health or accidents caused by tiredness. You should also have adequate breaks *(H&S Act 74)*.

To be a full-time trainee you have to attend training for 30 hours or more per seven-day period. Some trainees may be training part-time – your allowance may be reduced proportionately.

*Non-employed trainees*

You must not be asked to attend for more than 40 hours per week *(TEC PP, para C32.2.5)*. This 40 hours covers your time on work experience and on 'off-the-job' training. If the usual hours of work at your placement are less than 40 hours you should work the same hours as everyone else.

You may be asked to work weekends, evening or unusual hours if it is essential for training purposes, but the hours have to be agreed by you when you sign your ITP.

You cannot work 'overtime' as part of YT. If you want to work more than the agreed hours of training, an employer can employ you on a casual basis, doing work outside YT.

### Employed trainees

You may be asked to work more than 40 hours per week. Whatever hours you are expected to work should be recorded in your 'written terms and conditions of employment'.

## Holidays

### Non-employed trainees

It is up to TECs to agree with the Secretary of State what paid holidays trainees in their locality are entitled to.

In the past participants on YT and YTS had to be given a minimum of 19.5 days paid holiday per year (one and a half days per four weeks of training). In addition trainees were entitled to all Bank and Public Holidays or time off in lieu.

Your YT provider can give you more days than the minimum laid down by your local TEC and should do so where it is the practice of the sector or the industry in which you are being trained.

### Employed trainees

There is no legal minimum laid down for paid holidays, though current holiday levels are rarely less than four weeks per year.

Your written statement of terms and conditions of employment should state any entitlement to holidays, including Public Holidays, and holiday pay. It should state clearly the method by which your holiday entitlement is calculated so that when you leave you can work out what holiday pay is due. Your employer should give you Public Holidays or time off in lieu.

## Sickness

When you start YT you should be told the procedure to follow when you are absent due to sickness.

You need to get a doctor's certificate (sick note) if you are away for eight consecutive days or more, including Bank Holidays and weekends. Before then you must be covered by a doctor's certificate or self-certification for sickness, depending on what is acceptable to your YT provider.

### *Non-employed trainees*

If you are working alongside employees, the procedures to follow when you are absent due to sickness should be the same.

The length of time that your allowance will be paid if you are away sick is up to the TEC or LEC in your local area to decide. In the past trainees on YT and YTS continued to be paid their training allowance for up to 21 days of sickness absence.

If you have to leave YT because you are sick, your allowance is stopped. You may then be able to claim IS (see page 31) or your parents may be able to claim Child Benefit for you (see page 17).

### *Employed trainees*

Your written terms and conditions should set out what you must do if you are sick and what pay you will get. You may be eligible for Statutory Sick Pay or Sickness Pay or Sickness Benefit. Further details of these are given in the Child Poverty Action Group handbooks (see page xviii). If you lose your job because of sickness you may be able to claim IS (see page 31) or your parents may be able to claim Child Benefit for you (see page 17).

### *All trainees*

If you have to leave YT because of sickness you may be able to return to the same scheme when you recover, but you do not have an absolute right to do so. If you are under 18 you are covered by the YT

Guarantee and must be offered a place on YT (see page 82). If you have reached the age of 18 you are covered by the extended Guarantee and also have other options – see the *Unemployment and Training Rights Handbook* (details on page 149).

## Paid time off

Whether you get paid time off for things like interviews will be decided by your local TEC or LEC. All authorised absences should be paid for at the normal allowance rates.

In the past YT and YTS trainees were given time off, without deduction from their training allowance, for:
+ interviews for jobs or for advice on further training or education;
+ public examinations or to attend assessments of competence or tests;
+ court attendance and periods of training with Reserve and Cadet Forces;
+ up to three weeks compassionate leave;
+ up to three weeks where an industrial dispute that you are not involved in prohibits effective or safe training.

Whether you are an employed trainee or a non-employed trainee, if you are pregnant you should be given paid time off for antenatal care. This is a statutory entitlement for employees.

You need to agree time off in advance with your supervisor. You may not be paid for any time you are absent without permission. If you are absent without leave for 10 consecutive days (or less as laid down by your local TEC) you will be considered to have left Youth Training *(TEC PP, para C31.3)*.

## Trade union membership

Each TEC or LEC is able to establish its own policy with regard to trade union membership for non-employed trainees.

Employed trainees have the right to join a trade union *(EP Act 78)*. A dismissal is automatically unfair if it is because an employee joined, tried to join or took part in the activities of an independent trade union. You also have the right to complain to an industrial tribunal if your employer takes action which falls short of dismissal for membership of, or for taking part in the activities of, a union. If the industrial tribunal upholds the complaint it may award damages.

Many unions offer free membership or low rates for YT trainees.

Union representatives can advise you on issues such as health and safety, discrimination and the type of training being given. They also have experienced officials to represent you if you have a dispute with your scheme.

If you want to join, ask for details from your supervisor either at the scheme or at your workplace. If they cannot help, then contact your local Trades Council (in the Business telephone directory under Trade Unions).

## Grievance and disciplinary procedures: good practice

There are no longer any nationally imposed standards for grievance and disciplinary procedures for YT trainees. The minimum standards previously laid down in TEC contracts with the Government are outlined below. They serve as examples of the kind of good practice which may be stipulated by individual TECs at their discretion.

## Grievance procedures

Your local TEC or LEC determines the conditions for trainees covering grievance procedures.

### Non-employed trainees

The grievance procedure should be written down clearly and it should be explained to you when you start *(Hansard WA, 5/4/90, col 816)*. If you are not given your own copy of the grievance procedure, a copy should be kept somewhere you can easily go and see it.

If you have a problem or feel you are being unfairly treated you can discuss the matter with your supervisor. If the problem is not sorted out you can take it up with more senior management. You can take a friend, trade union representative or someone else with you.

At the TEC/LEC's discretion you can take your grievance to the TEC/LEC and also to the Careers Service once you have exhausted your scheme's procedures. TECs/LECs used to be obliged by the terms of their contracts to operate a complaints procedure, under which an individual with a complaint 'can be assured that his or her case will be duly considered by the chief executive of the TEC/LEC and if necessary by the chairman' *(Hansard WA, 14/5/89, col. 322)*.

If you are dissatisfied with the response you get from your TEC/LEC you can take your complaint further. In England you can take it directly to the DfEE or ask your MP to raise the issue with the Secretary of State for Education and Employment. In Scotland you can raise the issue with Scottish Enterprise or Highlands & Islands Enterprise or ask your MP to raise the issue with the Secretary of State for Scotland. In Wales you can raise the issue with the Welsh Office or ask your MP to raise the issue with the Secretary of State for Wales.

### Employed trainees

In your written statement of terms and conditions of employment you should have details of who you can go to if you have a problem, and the stages of the appeals procedure. If it doesn't spell out the details of the procedure you should be told where you can see them. They should be kept in a place which is readily accessible to you.

## Disciplinary procedures

Your local TEC decides the conditions for trainees covering disciplinary procedures.

### Non-employed trainees

When you start YT, the disciplinary procedures and any relevant agreements with trade unions should be explained to you *(Hansard WA, 5/4/90, col 816)*. Procedures should be clearly written down somewhere you can easily go and see them.

You have the right, at the TEC/LEC's discretion, to ask the TEC/LEC or Careers Service to consider a matter of discipline in connection with your training once you have gone through your scheme's procedures.

### Employed trainees

Employers with fewer than 20 employees no longer have to provide a written disciplinary procedure *(Emp Act 89, sec 13)*. However employees must still be given a note of any grievance procedures.

Larger employers should provide you with written details of disciplinary procedures. If they are not in your written statement of terms and conditions they must be kept where you can easily go and see them. They should include disciplinary rules and the person who you can go to if you are dissatisfied with a disciplinary decision.

### All trainees

You have the right to take a trade union representative or someone else (e.g. an advice worker or friend) in with you if you are going to be disciplined to take notes and support your case.

# Health and safety on YT

## Legal safeguards

Trainees on YT are entitled to the same protection under the law as an employed person in health and safety matters. Employers have a legal duty to ensure the health, safety and welfare of all their employees so far as is reasonably possible *(H&S Act 1974)*. Under the Health and Safety (Training for Employment) Regulations 1990, trainees in non-educational settings are treated as employees.

Note: Government requirements for TECs to monitor health and safety on YT are being reviewed. Until any changes are announced, standards from the 1996/7 *Annual Funding Agreement* (AFA) apply.

## Your right to safe working conditions

The TEC has to 'monitor health and safety provision to the degree and frequency determined by risk assessment but at least annually'. This must include 'sample visits down to placement level' *(AFA, para B4.1.2)*.

The law clearly states that you should not be exposed to risks to your health and safety. On some training schemes this duty has been ignored. Trainees have been injured at work; a number have been killed. Your life could depend on good health and safety practice.

It is your employer's duty to make sure you are properly trained and supervised, that equipment is maintained, and that gangways are kept clear. All possible hazards involved in your work should have been identified and either eliminated or controlled through the use of safety procedures or equipment.

It is your duty to obey safety rules. You also have a duty to other people with whom you work not to endanger their health or safety.

If you believe that where you work your employers are not carrying out their duties – or if you have any doubts about health and safety at work – you should report your worries to a trade union represent-ative, if one is available, or to the Careers Service, the local TEC or the local office of the Health and Safety Executive (see the phone book or ask in your local library).

You should refuse to do any job if you think it is unsafe, or if you haven't been trained to do it, or until you feel confident about what you are doing or have the necessary safety equipment.

## YT providers' obligations

YT providers and their sub-contractors have to comply with all relevant health and safety legislation and codes of practice approved by the Health and Safety Commission *(TEC Standards (draft), para C5.1)*.

The TEC must 'include suitable and sufficient health and safety clauses in its Provider Agreements covering at least the following 10 require-ments' *(AFA, para B4.1.1)*:
+ management of health and safety;
+ provision of safety policies and risk assessments;
+ staff competencies;
+ working environment;
+ equipment, materials and safe systems of work;
+ trainee training;
+ accident and disease investigation;
+ emergency planning;
+ contractual controls; and
+ vetting and monitoring.

The Management of Health and Safety Regulations 1992 require risk assessment in the workplace. This should cover such points as ensuring that you are provided with and use effectively any necessary protective clothing and equipment and that you get any necessary medical examinations. TEC/LECs may stipulate, as the national *TEC Operating Agreement* previously did, that non-employed trainees should not be charged for such clothing and equipment.

## Safety training

You should be given an advice booklet – *Be Safe!* – and guidance on relevant health and safety practices during induction and throughout your training. Safety training should be provided for all the jobs you are asked to do. For some jobs, you will need specific extra training or close supervision. *Be Safe!* is available free: telephone 01709 888688.

## Accidents

*Employed and non-employed trainees*
There should be an accident book and first aid facilities in the workplace. If you have an accident at work which results in an injury, however minor it appears to be, get it entered in the accident book. Write down exactly what happened and get any witnesses to do the same.

If you have a 'relevant' accident or an occupationally related disease, the TEC must ensure that a competent person investigates and completes an accident report form and returns it to the Government Office for the Region *(TEC PP, para B27.1)*.

Relevant accidents are defined as *(TEC PP, para B27.2)*:
✦ deaths;
✦ accidents resulting in injuries or conditions referred to in paragraph 3(2) of the Reporting of Injuries, Diseases and Dangerous Occurrences Regulations 1995 (SI 1995/3163);
✦ accidents resulting in you being absent from a programme for four consecutive days or more (including weekends, bank holidays and rest days but excluding the day of the accident);
✦ accidents resulting in any loss of physical or mental faculty or in disfigurement;
✦ any other accident which may give rise to a claim under the DfEE's Analogous Industrial Injuries Scheme (see below).

Non-accidental occurrences which result in injury and occupational diseases should also be reported and investigated.

## Industrial Injuries benefits

*Employed trainees*

If you are an employed trainee and have an accident which leaves you with a disability or you contract an industrial disease from your workplace you are entitled to claim benefits from the DSS under section 94 of the Social Security Contributions and Benefits Act 1992. If you have sufficient NI contributions you will receive Incapacity Benefit. Otherwise you will be eligible to make a claim for IS.

*Non-employed trainees*

If you are a non-employed trainee you should get a sick note from your doctor and claim Incapacity Benefit or IS from the Benefits Agency.

If after 14 weeks you are still affected by an injury or disease which was 'industrially' caused, you may be eligible to receive benefits from the DfEE under the Analogous Industrial Injuries Scheme (AIIS). These benefits do not depend on NI contributions. AIIS enables trainees to receive benefits for injuries received on Government training programmes. It operates under the same rules as the statutory scheme operated by the DSS and pays benefit at the same rates.

It is important that the appropriate documentation is completed as soon as an accident happens or an industrial disease is diagnosed.

If your claim is not accepted you will be given a full written explan-ation of the reasons. If you disagree with the rejection you have 21 days in which to present any fresh evidence that was not available at the time of the decision. The original decision will then be reviewed.

You can get more information about AIIS by writing to the Industrial Injuries Unit, Department for Education and Employment, Room N3, Moorfoot, Sheffield S1 4PQ or by telephoning free of charge on 0800 590395.

You may also have the right to sue the company where you work – you will need legal advice.

# Training allowances, tax and extra support

## The training allowance

### Non-employed trainees

You must receive at least the minimum training allowance. For 16 year olds the minimum weekly rate is £30 and for those aged 17 years or over it is £35. The higher rate is paid on and after your 17th birthday. Some TECs set higher minimums for their areas.

Generally you should receive your allowance weekly. If your YT provider has employees who are paid less frequently you may be paid at the same frequency. Your TEC or LEC has to ensure that payment is 'regular' *(TEC PP, para C31.2)*.

### Employed trainees

You do not have a minimum wage that you should receive. You should be given a pay slip which shows your wages before and after deductions for National Insurance, tax, etc.

You should be paid in the same way and at the same frequency as other employees.

### All trainees

The method of payment is decided by your YT provider/employer. This may be in cash, through bank or building society accounts, by Giro or otherwise.

### Advance payments

If the method of paying the allowance is likely to cause you financial hardship when you start YT your provider should consider making an interim (recoverable) advance payment. This could be necessary if, for instance, you have to pay rent for accommodation.

## Income Tax

*Non-employed trainees*

Youth Training allowances paid to young people who do not have employee status are not taxable *(Hansard WA, 17/2/95, col. 873)*.

*Employed Trainees*

Income tax has to be paid if your total income in a year is above the threshold. For a single person with no dependants for the tax year April 1997/April 1998 this threshold is £4,045. Any income over this threshold is taxable. The amount of the minimum training allowance is not excluded from this calculation.

Your employer or your training provider will normally deduct income tax at source for you unless you are self-employed.

## National Insurance

Paying National Insurance (NI) contributions entitles you to certain payments when you need them – for example, Contributory JSA, Maternity Allowance, Incapacity Benefit and a state pension.

NI contribution and eligibility rules are complex and you usually have to pay contributions in two calendar years ahead of being paid benefits. (For details see the CPAG's *Rights Guide to Non-Means-Tested Benefits.*)

*Non-employed trainees*

You do not pay NI contributions even if you get more than the minimum allowance *(Hansard WA, 17/2/95, col. 873)*.

Neither training providers nor employers providing work placements have any NI contribution liability for any young people with non-employed status on YT *(Hansard WA, 20/3/97, col. 897)*.

All young people are credited with Class 3 National Insurance contributions in the tax year in which they attain their sixteenth birthday and the two succeeding tax years. Class 3 contributions are for Retirement Pension and Widows' Benefit purposes.

Some young people may qualify for special NI credits to help them claim Incapacity Benefit or Contributory JSA after the end of their YT course. The conditions for getting these are strict and apply to only limited numbers of young people. The credits are awarded locally when a claim is made. They are not permanent credits and therefore are not noted on the person's NI account.

Some people on YT might benefit from 'approved training' credits, but not many as these apply only to people over 18 on a course of full-time training not intended to continue for more than 12 months.

### Employed trainees

You have to pay NI if you earn above a certain amount each week. In the tax year April 1977/April 1998 this is £62. If you earn less than this you will not be given any credits, but you can make voluntary contributions. Your employer should arrange for your NI contributions to be paid. If you fear that they are not being paid you can check through your local Benefits Agency office.

## Deductions

The TEC has to ensure that 'Trainees shall not be required to contribute financially to the cost of Training' *(TEC PP, para C30.4)*.

The only exceptions to this are:
+ payments taken from your Youth Credit;
+ if you have a Career Development Loan (see the *Unemployment and Training Rights Handbook* for more details);
+ where the Secretary of State agrees in advance that an individual contribution may be made.

Previously, your TEC/LEC had to ensure that your YT payment was not 'unreasonably' withheld and that deductions were not made 'unreasonably'. The only deductions that could be made from your allowance, if you were a non-employed trainee, were for:

✦ unauthorised absence;

✦ disciplinary reasons under established procedure;

✦ payments for necessary equipment, clothing or tools authorised by the TEC.

Individual TECs/LECs may still specify such safeguards at their discretion.

TECs are explicitly authorised to reduce the training allowance proportionately for part-time attendance and unauthorised absence *(TEC PP, para C31.2)*.

# Financial support from TECs

TECs/LECs have considerable flexibility in deciding whether to make additional payments to support trainees. However, they are obliged to meet some necessary costs (or arrange for training providers to do so) as explained below.

The TEC 'shall ensure that adequate support is available' to residents (see page 83) in the Guarantee Groups *(TEC PP, para C30.2)*:

✦ under the TEC's own contracts, wherever located;

✦ under another TEC's contract, provided such training arrangements have been agreed between the TECs concerned.

The TEC may provide support for all other residents under the TEC's own contracts *(TEC PP, para C30.3)*.

**Support** is defined as the help given to a person to enable them to take up and continue in training. It includes, but is not limited to, travelling expenses, accommodation expenses, the costs of tools, clothing and safety equipment, child care expenses and relevant assistance to people with disabilities *(TEC PP, C: Words and Expressions)*.

## Child care costs

TECs can pay child care costs to trainees on YT. They have to pay you child care costs if you could not join or continue in suitable training without reimbursement.

You may also be eligible for an Income Support top-up (see page 116).

## Extra support for people with a disability

Appropriate facilities and support should be available to enable you to join and benefit from YT if you have a disability.

You can ask about the various facilities available at your TEC/LEC. Your local Careers Service office and the Placement, Assessment and Counselling Team (PACT) at your nearest Jobcentre should also be able to help. Facilities and support provided through the TEC should cover at least such matters as:

◆ adaptations to premises or equipment;
◆ special aids or equipment;
◆ a readership service for the blind;
◆ an interpreter service for the deaf;
◆ individually tailored training programmes where existing contracted local provision is not appropriate in particular cases.

Where you need to retain a special aid in order to take up employment the TEC is expected to allow you to do so, by arrangement with the PACT.

## Travel costs

Whether or not you will be paid travel costs on top of your allowance is up to your local TEC or LEC or your training provider unless you would otherwise not be able to join or continue in training.

TEC/LECs and YT providers can agree to pay travel costs for trainees. In the past YT and YTS trainees were reimbursed the amount by which their weekly travel costs exceeded £3.

Your TEC/LEC should pay travel costs to you, or arrange for your training provider to pay travel costs, if not doing so would prevent you from joining or continuing in suitable training. However this is now at the discretion of the TEC/LEC.

If you are an *employed trainee* you do not have the right to have any weekly travel costs reimbursed, though some employers do pay for them.

*Lodging costs*

Lodging costs are paid at the discretion of TECs/LECs. However if you can join or continue in training only if they are met the TEC/LEC should arrange for your lodging costs to be paid.

Lodging costs can by paid to both *employed* and *non-employed* trainees. Trainees receiving lodging costs should also be paid for the return journey between home and lodgings and for 'occasional' visits home.

To award lodging costs the TEC/LEC will probably want to be satisfied that there is no local training opportunity of equivalent specification which would provide better value for money.

A lodging allowance can also be paid if your parents move and the TEC concludes that suitable training is not available in the new 'home' area or that a change of training location would jeopardise your progress.

# State and local authority benefits on YT

## Income Support top-ups

The payment of IS top-ups has been very poorly publicised. However the extra money plus the passport to other benefits (see below) could make a huge financial difference.

### Living away from home

If you are a non-employed trainee you can claim IS (Category (b) on page 30). IS will pay the difference between your YT allowance and what you would get if you were on IS. The YT allowance is normally higher than the personal allowance allowed under IS, so that normally you would *not* be eligible for an IS top-up.

However, the higher rate of the single person allowance for 16 and 17 year olds (£38.90) is greater than the minimum YT allowance for 16 year olds (£30) and for 17 year olds (£35). If you have a 'good reason' for living away from home you are therefore entitled to £8.90 or £3.90 IS on top of your allowance. These are the same 'good reasons' as those which apply to certain JSA applicants (see page 35).

### 18–24 year olds

If you are aged 18–24 your IS allowance is £38.90 even if you live at home. So if you are over 18 and a non-employed trainee on YT getting the minimum allowance you can claim £3.90 IS.

### Trainees with children

If you are a non-employed trainee and have a child or children you may be entitled to an IS top-up. This may be the case even if you are not on the minimum allowance, whether or not you live with your parents and whether you are single or in a couple. You make a claim at your local Benefits Agency. (Non-employed trainees are also entitled to the IS premiums for having a disabled child and carers.)

*Passported benefits*

Entitlement to IS will also passport you to maximum Housing Benefit, Council Tax Benefit (some 18 year olds can be liable for Council Tax), Social Fund payments (including community care grants, budgeting loans and maternity expenses), exemption from health charges (including prescriptions and charges for dental treatment) and vouchers towards glasses.

## Housing Benefit

If you are living away from your family and have responsibility for paying rent you can apply to the local authority for Housing Benefit to help cover the cost of your rent. This applies whether you are an employed or non-employed trainee.

## Disability Living Allowance

DLA has a mobility component and a care component. Taking part in YT may affect your entitlement to the care component. Participation in YT can be viewed as a change in your circumstances and the care component could be reviewed on that basis. Starting training may suggest that you now have fewer care needs or that you now need less assistance/supervision from another person.

After six months on a scheme, you will be asked whether your needs have changed. Depending on your answer, your DLA may be reviewed. If your needs are unchanged you should have little to worry about. If you are unsure if your care needs have changed or if you are receiving the highest rate of care component, seek advice before you contact the DLA Unit.

## Severe Disablement Allowance (SDA)

SDA is a weekly cash benefit for people who have been incapable of work for at least 28 weeks but who do not have enough National Insurance contributions to qualify for Incapacity Benefit.

16 and 17 year olds who receive SDA and who also claim IS will be paid IS at the higher rate together with the disability premium. This means their IS entitlement may exceed their SDA and they will be paid the difference as IS.

You have to give up SDA on starting a YT course. This is because a day when you receive a training allowance cannot count as a day when you are incapable of work. You can claim disability premium as outlined below.

### *Reclaiming SDA after YT*

Some young people have been discouraged from taking up YT because, if the training is unsuccessful and does not lead to a job, they may not be able to reclaim SDA when they leave.

Normally, if you have completed a YT programme, this would be taken as evidence that you are capable of work – and so not eligible for SDA. However, an adjudication officer can still decide that, despite completing a course, you are incapable of work.

If you are unable to work when the course ends because of illness or disability you can pick up SDA again if you are accepted as incapable of work. SDA can be reinstated immediately, because the claim links with earlier entitlement.

You must claim SDA **the day after your training finishes** for the claims to link. If they do not link you will have to be incapable of work for another 28 weeks before you can claim.

## Disability premium

Though you lose SDA when you join YT, you are still treated as incapable of work for the purposes of the disability premium, and so retain the right to this payment if you are non-employed.

You cannot qualify for the premium on the grounds of incapacity for work while on YT unless you were previously entitled to SDA.

Non-employed trainees in this situation who are paid the minimum training allowance can claim from their local Benefits Agency a significant top-up to their training allowance, whether they have left home or not.

A 16-year-old non-employed trainee on the minimum allowance who is entitled to the disability premium can claim a supplement of £29.85 a week to her/his training allowance from April 1997 to April 1998. A 17-year-old non-employed trainee on £35.00 a week can claim a top-up of £24.85 a week.

Getting IS also gives you the right to other benefits such as maximum Housing Benefit, Council Tax Benefit (for those 18 year olds who are liable for Council Tax), Social Fund payments, and free prescriptions and dental treatment.

# MODERN APPRENTICESHIPS

## What are Modern Apprenticeships?

The Modern Apprenticeships programme is designed to provide a limited number of young people with training which leads to a qualification at or above NVQ level 3 or equivalent. Modern Apprenticeships have been developed by lead TECs in conjunction with Industry Training Organisations (ITOs) for particular occupational sectors. How they operate will vary between occupational sectors.

The training delivered under Modern Apprenticeships must conform to the national framework for its sector, including employed-status where this is specified. A TEC must register its local scheme with the relevant ITO. The term 'Modern Apprenticeship' must be used, and can only be used, where the local scheme has been registered in this way and uses Modern Apprenticeship funding *(AFA, para B27)*.

In Scotland, the employer or training provider registers with the ITO to use its framework.

## The aims of Modern Apprenticeships

The stated aims of Modern Apprenticeships are that TECs/LECs shall aim to provide an Apprenticeship to eligible people which leads to at least NVQ level 3 which shall *(AFA, para B26)*:

◆ be appropriate to the needs and abilities of the individual;
◆ take account of local labour market circumstances; and
◆ conform to the framework agreed by the Modern Apprenticeship National Steering Group for the sector concerned (in Scotland, the Modern Apprenticeship Implementation Group).

# Eligibility, the Guarantee and access

Eligibility for Modern Apprenticeships is the same as for YT *(TEC PP, para C19)*. The TEC's obligations under the YT Guarantee can be met by placing you in a Modern Apprenticeship *(TEC PP, para C20.2)*. The Guarantee Groups and rules regarding them are the same for YT and Modern Apprenticeships.

You must have a Youth Credit (in Scotland, Skillseekers) to take up a Modern Apprenticeship. The programme is run through Youth Credits/Skillseekers arrangements *(TEC PP, para C18.1)*.

The TEC has to ensure that 'an Apprentice shall not be required to contribute financially to the cost of the Apprenticeship' *(TEC PP, para C40.3)*. The only exceptions to this are using your Youth Credit and using a Career Development Loan (see the *Unemployment and Training Rights Handbook* for more details) or where the Secretary of State agrees in advance that you may make an individual contribution.

You must not be refused access to Modern Apprenticeships on the grounds that you are not resident in the TEC's area.

# Assessment

You must be assessed before or on joining Modern Apprenticeships *(TEC PP, para C39.1)*.

## Special training needs

If you are assessed as suitable for a Modern Apprenticeship and have special training needs you must receive relevant extra help to enable you to progress towards NVQ level 3 or higher *(TEC PP, para C39.2)*.

## Apprenticeship Plan

You must be given an Apprenticeship Plan agreed by you within two weeks (four weeks in Wales) of starting. It must be such that you have a reasonable prospect of completing it successfully within the duration it specifies *(TEC PP, para C42)*. It should include *(TEC PP, para C42.2):*

✦ your name and signature;

✦ your prior learning and assessed needs;

✦ a statement that the Apprenticeship Plan is to be carried out under Modern Apprenticeship arrangements – you must have unrestricted access to information on the arrangements;

✦ the start date for training, and the intended leaving date;

✦ the attendance requirements, which should be at least 16 hours a week, and for non-employed apprentices a maximum of 40 hours a week;

✦ any agreed support arrangements;

✦ the name, level and reference number of at least one qualification which you aim to achieve, at NVQ level 3 or higher standard;

✦ a list of all the units which together make up the NVQ and the time scales in which these are likely to be achieved;

✦ the core additions relating to the acquisition of transferable skills which will be achieved during the Apprenticeship;

✦ how units of the NVQ and the core additions will be assessed and learnt;

✦ your employment or career objectives.

The Apprenticeship Plan must be underwritten by a Training Agreement *(TEC PP, para C42.4)*. This should be signed within two weeks (13 weeks in Wales) of your starting the Apprenticeship by you, an employer, and a representative of the TEC. The Training Agreement will express the commitment of those signing to the successful completion of the Apprenticeship. You should keep a copy.

The Apprenticeship Plan and your progress against it must be kept under regular review *(TEC PP, para C43.1)*. If special training needs have been mentioned in your Apprenticeship Plan, the review must evaluate how far extra help is successfully addressing those needs.

*Dissatisfaction with the Apprenticeship Plan*

Your Apprenticeship Plan may be changed during your training, but only with your agreement. If you express reasonable dissatisfaction with the delivery of your Plan or if, in the opinion of the TEC or your employer/training provider, you are no longer making satisfactory progress, you should be offered an alternative Apprenticeship or Youth Training with the same employer/provider or another employer/provider on the basis of a new Apprenticeship Plan or Individual Training Plan *(TEC PP, para C43.2)*.

Any change to your existing Apprenticeship or any transfer to another employer/provider must be agreed by you. However if you 'unreasonably withhold' your consent, you may be required to discontinue your Apprenticeship *(TEC PP, para C43.2)*.

If the employer/provider can no longer provide the Apprenticeship in accordance with your Apprenticeship Plan, for example because of closing down, the TEC has to ensure that you are offered the opportunity to transfer, with a substantially similar Apprenticeship Plan or an alternative Individual Training Plan, to another employer/provider *(TEC PP, para C43.3)*.

Many Training Agreements also commit the employer or ITO to helping you find alternative training in the sector.

## Training records

You should be given a National Record of Achievement (NRA) when you start your Apprenticeship if you do not already have one. Your NRA should be kept up to date *(TEC PP, para C44)*.

## Terms and conditions

In almost all respects, your rights on a Modern Apprenticeship are the same as on YT (see pages 96–109.) This includes terms and conditions, the requirements that you receive adequate support, health and safety provisions and your eligibility to training allowances and other payments. The only difference is that if your employer/provider can no longer provide the Apprenticeship, you can be offered a transfer to a similar Apprenticeship Plan or an *alternative* Individual Training Plan, as noted above.

The minimum training allowance for non-employed apprenticeships is the same as the YT allowance: £30 for 16 year olds and £35 for 17 year olds.

# Accelerated Modern Apprenticeships

Accelerated Modern Apprenticeships became nationally available from September 1995. They were designed to offer training to NVQ level 3 or equivalent to people aged between 18 and 20 who stayed on at school after the minimum school leaving age.

In April 1996 Accelerated Modern Apprenticeships were merged with Modern Apprenticeships to form a single Modern Apprenticeship programme governed by Modern Apprenticeship planning, funding and contracting arrangements.

In Wales, Accelerated Modern Apprenticeships are available to young people who have already achieved NVQ level 2 (or equivalent) or who have left full-time education and are able to complete their training before their 25th birthday. All Accelerated Modern Apprentices will have employed-status from the outset and apprentices will normally be expected to complete their training within two years of starting.

# NATIONAL TRAINEESHIPS

The 1996 Education and Training White Paper, *Learning to Compete*, announced that National Traineeships would be introduced. They will offer a work-based route to qualifications *(TEC PP, para C15.1)*. They are scheduled to be phased in from September 1997.

The main differences from YT are to be *(TEC PP, para C15.2)*:
✦ a focus on NVQ and key skills at level 2;
✦ involvement of sectors of industry and commerce in the design of training;
✦ a requirement for individual employers to be directly involved in training delivery.

DfEE guidance on the conversion of planned YT starts to National Traineeship starts 'will follow' *(TEC PP, para C3.1)*.

# RELAUNCH

Relaunch was also announced in *Learning to Compete*. It is *(TEC PP, para C16.1)*: 'a national strategy based upon partnership projects which co-ordinate local action to tackle poor motivation and non-participation in learning'. It is planned to start from September 1997.

In Wales it will be called Youth Access Initiative and will begin to operate from 1998/99, with the purpose of stepping up action to reintegrate disaffected young people into education, training and jobs.

# A NOTE ON FOYERS AND
## OTHER TRAINING PROGRAMMES

Foyers link accommodation (usually in hostels) to training and employment. They have been piloted as a new initiative in certain areas.

Special conditions for some training programmes apply to residents of the YMCA pilot foyers in Nottingham, Norwich, St Helens, Romford and Wimbledon. If you are a resident of one of these you have exemption from the basic eligibility conditions for Jobclub, Job Interview Guarantee, Job Search Seminars and Work Trials. The minimum age for joining these programmes is only 17 for residents of these foyers, instead of 18. Also you can join one of these programmes on or after your first day of unemployment, instead of having to wait for a qualifying period. However, the Government's Guarantee of a YT place still applies, and you must first have been offered a place on YT. You do not have to have accepted the YT offer, but your education and training options must have been fully explored by your local TEC.

For information about Jobclub, Job Interview Guarantee, Job Search Seminars and Work Trials, see the *Unemployment and Training Rights Handbook* (see page 149).

# *APPENDIX A*
# APPROVED QUALIFICATIONS

Approved qualifications are central elements of YT and Modern Apprenticeships. All YT trainees (with the exception of some trainees with special training needs) should be in training which leads to at least one approved qualification at or above National Vocational Qualification (NVQ) level 2 standard *(TEC PP, para C32.2.7)*. Young people in Modern Apprenticeships should be in training which leads to at least NVQ level 3 *(TEC PP, para C42.2.7)*. A percentage of the funding TECs and LECs receive from the Government for YT, Modern Apprenticeships and Youth Credits is dependent on trainees gaining approved qualifications.

An approved qualification is *(TEC PP, C: Words and expressions)*:
+ a qualification approved as an NVQ;
+ any forerunner qualification contained in the Vocational Qualifications Listings of acceptable qualifications;
+ a General National Vocational Qualification (GNVQ);
+ an educational qualification;
+ a foundation level Wordpower or Numberpower qualification;
+ an Access to Higher Education Certificate.

## National Council for Vocational Qualifications

The National Council for Vocational Qualifications (NCVQ) was set up by the Government in 1986 to design a simple and coherent system of vocational qualifications across all occupations at all levels. So far there are 858 NVQs covering 85% of the employed population.

The Council's remit extends to England, Northern Ireland and Wales, but not to Scotland. In Scotland SCOTVEC is undertaking a similar function to NCVQ. The equivalent of NVQs in Scotland are Scottish Vocational Qualifications (SVQs).

## Lead bodies

Although NCVQ is the main player in the system, several others are involved. 'Lead bodies' have been created for individual occupational areas. There are over a hundred of these employer-dominated bodies, which take responsibility for producing the occupational standards. In some cases there was either an Industrial Training Board or a major Non-Statutory Training Organisation to act as a focus for the work. In other areas, e.g. business, administration and clerical occupations, a consortium had to be put together.

## Awarding bodies

The awarding bodies (principally City & Guilds, RSA and BTEC) use the new standards as the basis for vocational qualifications which they then present to NCVQ for accreditation as NVQs. To be accredited, the vocational qualifications must comply with NCVQ criteria.

## Criteria

NCVQ has laid stress on designing criteria which all NVQs must meet and which aim to improve access to vocational qualifications.

Each NVQ is made up of 'units of competence' which are required to do a job. These are divided into 'elements' and each element has a number of 'performance criteria' and 'range variables' which are used by the candidate and the assessor to determine competence. Units of competence can be collected gradually, working towards a full NVQ.

Assessment for NVQs is by demonstration of competence required to satisfy performance criteria – preferably in the workplace.

There should be no constraints on mode or duration of delivery or on age. Assessment is about whether you meet the standards of competence, not about how you got to that standard.

Assessment should also only assess what it's supposed to be assessing and not additional skills. For example, you should not be asked to show a higher level of reading skills than you need to do the job being assessed. Beyond that there must be no discriminatory practices – either overt or covert – including those relating to any groups with special needs.

Technically NCVQ's concept of competence involves skills which ensure that people can cope with change, transfer and progress. There are, however, fears that lead bodies are being too job-specific – meeting employers' immediate needs rather than the longer-term needs of a trained workforce.

## Framework of NVQ levels

The ultimate aim is not only that people should be more appropriately qualified, but also that more people should be qualified and be more highly qualified by being able to progress through a unified, recognised system. Therefore NCVQ has created a framework for vocational qualifications. Initially it had four levels from basic practical competence at work (level 1) to approximately the current Higher National Diplomas/higher technician level (level 4); level 5 has now been added.

Every NVQ has to be allocated to one of the levels and there is, in theory, comparability across all occupations at each level, although in practice there are concerns about the different demands of NVQs within the same level.

The levels are defined as follows:

Level 1    competence in the performance of a range of varied work activities, most of which may be routine and predictable.

Level 2    competence in a significant range of varied work activities, performed in a variety of contexts. Some of the activities are complex or non-routine, and there is some individual responsibility or autonomy. Collaboration with others, perhaps through membership of a work group or team, may often be a requirement.

Level 3    competence in a broad range of varied work activities performed in a wide variety of contexts and most of which are complex and non-routine. There is considerable responsibility and autonomy, and control or guidance of others is often required.

Level 4    competence in a broad range of complex, technical or professional work activities performed in a wide variety of contexts and with a substantial degree of personal responsibility and autonomy. Responsibility for the work of others and the allocation of resources is often present.

Level 5    competence which involves the application of a significant range of fundamental principles across a wide and often unpredictable variety of contexts. Very substantial personal autonomy and often significant responsibility for the work of others and for the allocation of substantial resources feature strongly, as do personal accountabilities for analysis and diagnosis, design, planning, execution and evaluation.

## Equivalent qualifications

As the process of accrediting NVQs is not yet complete, the DfEE issues TECs with a list of 'equivalent qualifications' that YT and Modern Apprenticeships should provide until an appropriate NVQ is available. For more details about equivalent qualifications contact your local TEC/LEC.

## Educational qualifications

You can study for educational qualifications on YT and Modern Apprenticeships provided they are relevant to your career objective and are part of a longer-term objective to achieve an NVQ (or equivalent) or a GNVQ (see below) in your chosen occupational area. The NVQ or GNVQ does not necessarily have to be achieved within your time on YT or Modern Apprenticeship, using your Youth Credit. The educational qualification has to be regarded as educationally equivalent to an NVQ at a given level. This is how the TEC's output-related funding will be worked out. The following equivalences apply *(TEC PP, C: Words and Expressions)*:

| Educational qualifications | NVQ equivalents |
| --- | --- |
| 3 GCSEs at any grade | one at level 1 |
| 4 GCSEs grade C or above | one at level 2 |
| 1 A level | one at level 2 |
| 2 AS levels | one at level 2 |
| 2 A levels | one at level 3 |
| 4 AS levels | one at level 3 |
| 1 A plus 2 AS levels | one at level 3 |
| Access to Higher Education Certificate | one at level 3 |

For young people in special training needs category B only (see page 93), the achievement of 3 GCSEs (irrespective of grade) will be deemed equivalent to the achievement of NVQ level 1 for payment purposes.

The award of an Access to Higher Education Certificate shall be deemed the equivalent of an NVQ level 3 for payment purposes.

## General National Vocational Qualifications

NCVQ, with the awarding bodies and professional and employer organisations, has developed General National Vocational Qualifications (GNVQs). GNVQs provide a third choice, alongside academic qualifications and NVQs. They are intended to allow young people to study for vocational qualifications which prepare them for a range of related occupations without limiting their choices too early. They are in part a response to criticism that NVQs are too occupationally specific. Scotland has a similar system, GSVQs.

There are three levels of GNVQ: Foundation, Intermediate and Advanced. Intermediate is comparable to GCSE standard and Advanced to A level for purposes of progression in education.

GNVQs aim to:
- ✦ offer a broad preparation for employment as well as an accepted route to higher level qualifications, including higher education;
- ✦ develop core skills – those which employers require in the workplace – including application of number and communication and the use of information technology;
- ✦ be of equal standing with academic qualifications at the same level.

## National Record of Achievement

The National Record of Achievement (NRA) is a record, in summary form, of your achievements: academic, vocational and other achievements such as work experience or voluntary or community work. The NRA 'is a life-long record of an individual's progress of achievements through schools, further and higher education, training organisations and in employment' *(TEC PP, C: Words and expressions)*.

TECs have to ensure that, if you do not have a copy of the NRA when you join YT or a Modern Apprenticeship, you are given one as soon as possible. The NRA must be kept up to date during your training *(TEC PP, para C35)*. The NRA is a UK national document for young people in England, Wales, Scotland and Northern Ireland.

## Further information

For details about NVQs and GNVQs generally contact:
NCVQ Publications, 222 Euston Road, London NW1 2EF
Phone: 0171 387 9898

For details about SVQs contact:
SCOTVEC, Hanover House, 24 Douglas Street, Glasgow G2 7NQ
Phone: 0141 248 7900

# APPENDIX B
# ADDRESSES OF TECs AND LECs

## 1: TECs by region

### EAST MIDLANDS

**Greater Nottingham TEC**                                **0115 941 3313**
Marina Rd, Castle Marina Park, Nottingham NG7 1TN

**Leicestershire TEC**                                    **0116 265 1515**
Meridian East, Meridian Business Park, Leicester LE3 2WZ

**Lincolnshire TEC**                                      **01522 567765**
Beech House, Witham Park, Waterside South, Lincoln LN5 7JQ

**Northamptonshire Chamber of Commerce, Training &**
**Enterprise**                                            **01604 671200**
Royal Pavilion, Summerhouse Rd, Moulton Park Industrial Estate,
Northampton NN3 6BJ

**North Derbyshire TEC**                                  **01246 551158**
Block C, St Mary's Court, St Mary's Gate, Chesterfield S41 7TD

**North Nottinghamshire TEC**                             **01623 824624**
1st Floor, Block C, Edwinstone House, High St, Edwinstone, Mansfield
NG21 9PR

**Southern Derbyshire Chamber of Commerce, Training &**
**Enterprise**                                            **01332 290550**
St Helen's Court, St Helen's St, Derby DE1 3GY

### EASTERN

**Bedfordshire TEC**                                      **01234 843100**
Woburn Court, 2 Railton Rd, Woburn Rd Industrial Estate, Kempston
MK42 7PN

**CAMBSTEC (Central & South Cambridgeshire)    01223 235633/635**
Unit 2-3, Trust Court, Chivers Way, The Vision Park, Histon, Cambridge
CB4 4PW

**Essex TEC                                                    01245 450123**
Redwing House, Hedgerows Business Park, Colchester Rd, Chelmsford
CM2 5PB

**Greater Peterborough TEC                        01733 890808**
Stuart House, City Road, Peterborough PE1 1QF

**Hertfordshire TEC                                      01727 813600**
45 Grosvenor Rd, St Albans, Hertfordshire AL1 3AW

**Norfolk & Waveney TEC                          01603 763812**
Partnership House, Unit 10, Norwich Business Park, Whiting Rd, Norwich
NR4 6DJ

**Suffolk TEC                                                01743 218951**
2nd Floor, Crown House, Crown St, Ipswich IP1 3HS

# LONDON

**Aztec                                                          0181 547 3934**
Manorgate House, 2 Manorgate Rd, Kingston upon Thames KT2 7AL

**Focus Central London Ltd** (address not yet known). Merger between:
**CENTEC (Central London)                        0171 411 3500**
12 Grosvenor Crescent, London SW1X 7EE, and
**CILNTEC (City and Inner London North) 0171 324 2424)**
80 Great Eastern St, London EC2A 3DP

**LETEC (London East TEC)                        0171 377 1866**
Cityside House, 40 Adler St., London E1 1EE

**North London TEC                                    0181 447 9422**
Dumayne House, 1 Fox Lane, Palmers Green, London N13 4AB

**North West London TEC                          0181 424 8866**
Kirkfield House, 118-120 Station Rd, Harrow, Middlesex HA1 2RL

**SOLOTEC                                          .          0181 313 9232**
Lancaster House, 7 Elmfield Rd, Bromley, Kent BR1 1LT

**West London TEC   ,                                0181 577 1010**
Sovereign Court, 15-21 Staines Rd, Hounslow, Middlesex TW3 3HA   ·

# MERSEYSIDE

**CEWTEC (Chester, Ellesmere Port & Wirral)**     **0151 650 0555**
Egerton House, 2 Tower Rd, Birkenhead, Wirral L41 1FN

**Merseyside TEC**     **0151 236 0026**
3rd Floor, Tithebarn House, Tithebarn St, Liverpool L2 2NZ

**St Helens Chamber of Commerce, Training &**
**Enterprise**     **01744 742000**
7 Waterside Court, Technology Campus, St Helens, Merseyside WA9 1UE

# NORTH EAST

**County Durham TEC**     **01325 351166**
Valley St North, Darlington DL1 1TJ

**Northumberland TEC**     **01670 713303**
Suite 2, Craster Court, Manor Walk Shopping Centre, Cramlington
NE23 6XX

**Sunderland City TEC**     **0191 516 0222**
Business & Innovation Centre, Sunderland Enterprise Park, Wearfield,
Sunderland SR5 2TA

**Teesside TEC**     **01642 231023**
Training and Enterprise House, 2 Queens Square, Middlesborough,
Cleveland TS2 1AA

**Tyneside TEC**     **0191 491 6000**
Moongate House, 5th Avenue Business Park, Team Valley Trading Estate
NE11 0HF

# NORTH WEST

**Bolton/Bury TEC**     **01204 397350**
Clive House, Clive St, Bolton BL1 1ET

**Cumbria TEC**     **01900 66991**
Venture House, Regents Court, Guard St, Workington, Cumbria CA14 4EW

**ELTEC (East Lancashire)**     **01254 301333**
Red Rose Court, Petre Rd, Clayton Business Park, Clayton-Le-Moor, Lancs
BB5 5JR

**LAWTEC (Lancashire Area West)**     **01772 792111**
Caxton Road, Fulwood, Preston PR2 9ZB

| | |
|---|---|
| **Manchester TEC** | **0161 236 7222** |
| Lee House, 90 Great Bridgewater St, Manchester M1 5JW | |
| **METROTEC (Wigan)** | **01942 705705** |
| The Investment Centre, Waterside Drive, Wigan WN3 5BA | |
| **NORMIDTEC (North & Mid Cheshire)** | **01925 826515** |
| Spencer House, Dewhurst Rd, Birchwood, Warrington WA3 7PP | |
| **Oldham Chamber of Commerce, Training & Enterprise** | **0161 620 0006** |
| Meridian Centre, King St, Oldham OL8 1EZ | |
| **Rochdale TEC** | **01706 44909** |
| St James Place, 160-162 Yorkshire St, Rochdale OL16 2DL | |
| **South & East Cheshire TEC** | **01606 737009** |
| PO Box 37, Middlewich Industrial & Business Park, Dalton Way, Middlewich CW10 0HU | |
| **Stockport/High Peak TEC** | **0161 477 8830** |
| 1 St Peter's Square, Stockport, SK1 1NN | |

# SOUTH EAST

| | |
|---|---|
| **Hampshire TEC** | **01329 230099** |
| 25 Thackeray Mall, Fareham, Hampshire, PO16 0PQ | |
| **Heart of England TEC** | **01235 553249** |
| 26/27 The Quadrant, Abingdon Science Park, Off Barton Lane, Abingdon, OX14 3YS | |
| **Kent TEC** | **01732 220000** |
| 26 Kings Hill Avenue, Kings Hill, West Malling, Kent ME19 4TA | |
| **Milton Keynes and North Bucks Chamber of Commerce, Training & Enterprise** | **01908 660002** |
| Tempus, 249 Midsummer Boulevard, Central Milton Keynes, MK9 1EU | |
| **Surrey TEC** | **01483 728190** |
| Technology House, 48-54 Goldsworth Rd, Woking, Surrey, GU21 1LE | |
| **Sussex Enterprise** | **01444 259259** |
| Greenacre Court, Station Rd, Burgess Hill, W Sussex, RH15 9DS | |
| **Thames Valley Enterprise** | **01734 568156** |
| 6th Floor, Kings Point, 120 Kings Rd, Reading, RG1 3BZ | |
| **Wight Training and Enterprise** | **01983 822818** |
| Mill Court, Furrlongs, Newport, Isle of Wight, PO30 2AA | |

# SOUTH WEST

**Devon & Cornwall TEC**      **01752 767929**
Foliot House, Brooklands, Budshead Rd, Crownhill, Plymouth, PL6 5XR

**Dorset TEC**      **01202 299284**
25 Oxford Rd, Bournemouth, BH8 8EY

**Gloucestershire TEC**      **01452 524488**
Conway House, 33-35 Worcester St, Gloucester, GL1 3AJ

**Somerset TEC**      **01823 321188**
East Reach House, East Reach, Taunton, Somerset, TA1 3EN

**WESTEC (formerly Avon)**      **0117 927 7116**
P.O. Box 164, St Lawrence House, 29-31 Broad St, Bristol, BS99 7HR

**Wiltshire TEC**      **01793 513644**
The Bora Building, Westlea Campus, Westlea Down, Swindon, Wiltshire, SN5 7EZ

# WALES

**Gwent TEC**      **01633 817777**
Glyndwr House, Unit B2, Cleppa Park, Newport, Gwent, NP1 9BA

**Mid Glamorgan TEC**      **01443 841594**
Unit 17-20 Centre Court, Main Avenue, Treforest Industrial Estate, Pontypridd, Mid-Glamorgan, CF37 5YL

**North Wales TEC**      **01745 585400**
(merger of TARGED/North West Wales TEC and North East Wales TEC)
Unit 7, St Asaph Business Park, St Asaph, Denbighshire, LL17 0LJ

**Powys TEC**      **01686 622494**
1st Floor, St David's House, Newtown, Powys, SY16 1RB

**South Glamorgan TEC**      **01222 451000**
3-7 Drake Walk, Brigantine Place, Atlantic Wharf, Cardiff CF1 5AN

**West Wales TEC**      **01792 354000**
3rd Floor, Orchard House, Orchard St, Swansea, West Glamorgan, SA1 5DJ

# WEST MIDLANDS

**Birmingham TEC**      **0121 622 4419**
Chaplin Court, 80 Hurst St, Birmingham B5 4TG

| | |
|---|---|
| **Central England TEC** | **01527 545415** |
| The Oaks, Clewes Rd, Redditch B98 7ST | |
| **Coventry & Warwickshire TEC** | **01203 635666** |
| Brandon Court, Progress Way, Coventry CV3 2TE | |
| **Dudley TEC** | **01384 485000** |
| Dudley Court South, Waterfront East, Level St, Brierley Hill, West Midlands DY5 1NX | |
| **HAWTEC (Hereford & Worcester)** | **01905 723200** |
| Haswell House, St Nicholas St, Worcester, WR1 1UW | |
| **Sandwell TEC** | **0121 543 2222** |
| 1st Floor Black Country House, Rounds Green Road, Oldbury, Warley, West Midlands, B69 2DG | |
| **Shropshire TEC** | **01952 208200** |
| Trevithick House, Stafford Park 4, Telford TF3 3BA | |
| **Staffordshire TEC** | **01782 202733** |
| Festival Way, Festival Park, Stoke on Trent, Staffordshire ST1 5TQ | |
| **Walsall TEC** | **01922 32332** |
| 5th Floor, Townend House, Townend Square, Walsall WS1 1NS | |
| **Wolverhampton TEC** | **01902 397787** |
| Pendeford Business Park, Wobaston Rd, Wolverhampton WV9 5HA | |

# YORKSHIRE AND HUMBERSIDE

| | |
|---|---|
| **Barnsley/Doncaster TEC** | **01226 248088** |
| Conference Centre, Eldon St, Barnsley S70 2JL | |
| **Bradford & District TEC** | **01274 751333** |
| Mercury House, 4 Manchester Road, Bradford BD5 0QL | |
| **Calderdale & Kirklees TEC** | **01484 400770** |
| Park View House, Woodvale Office Park, Woodvale Rd, Brighouse HD6 4AB | |
| **Humberside TEC** | **01482 226491** |
| The Maltings, Silvester Square, Silvester St, Hull HU1 3HL | |
| **Leeds TEC** | **0113 234 7666** |
| Belgrave Hall, Belgrave St, Leeds LS2 8DD | |
| **North Yorkshire TEC** | **01904 691939** |
| TEC House, 7 Pioneer Business Park, Amy Johnson Way, Clifton Moorgate, York, YO3 8TN | |

| | |
|---|---|
| **Rotherham TEC** | **01709 830511** |
| Moorgate House, 23 Moorgate Rd, Rotherham S60 2EN | |
| **Sheffield TEC** | **0114 270 1911** |
| St Mary's Court, 55 St Mary's Rd, Sheffield S2 4AQ | |
| **Wakefield TEC** | **01924 299907** |
| Grove Hall, 60 College Grove Rd, Wakefield WF1 3RN | |

# 2. LECs

## HIGHLANDS & ISLANDS ENTERPRISE

**Argyll and the Islands Enterprise**           **01546 602281**
The Enterprise Centre, Kilmory Industrial Estate, Lochgilphead, Argyll
PA31 8SH

**Caithness and Sutherland Enterprise**           **01847 896115**
Scapa House, Castlegreen Rd, Thurso, Caithness KW14 7LS

**Inverness and Nairn Enterprise**           **01463 713504**
Castle Wynd, Inverness IV3 3DW

**Lochaber Ltd**           **01397 704326**
St Mary's House, Gordon Square, Fort William PH33 6DY

**Moray, Badenoch and Strathspey Enterprise Co**
(Joint responsibility of Highlands & Islands Enterprise
and Scottish Enterprise)           **01343 550567**
Unit 14-17, Elgin Business Centre, Maisondieu Rd, Elgin IV30 1RH

**Orkney Enterprise**           **01856 874638**
14 Queen St, Kirkwall, Orkney KW15 1JE

**Ross & Cromarty Enterprise**           **01349 853666**
62 High St, Invergordon IV18 0DH

**Shetland Enterprise**           **01595 693177**
Toll Clock Shopping Centre, 26 North Rd, Lerwick, Shetland ZE1 0PE

**Skye and Lochalsh Enterprise**           **01478 612841**
Kings House, The Green, Portree, Isle of Skye IV51 9BS

**Western Isles Enterprise**           **01851 703703**
3 Harbour View, Cromwell St Quay, Stornoway, Isle of Lewis HS1 2DF

# SCOTTISH ENTERPRISE

**Dumfries & Galloway Enterprise**                    01387 245000
Solway House, Dumfries Enterprise Park, Tinwald Downs Rd, Dumfries
DG1 3SJ

**Dunbartonshire Enterprise**                    0141 951 2121
2nd Floor, Spectrum House, Clydebank Business Park, Clydebank, Glasgow
G81 2DR

**Enterprise Ayrshire**                    01563 526623
17-19 Hill St, Kilmarnock, Ayrshire KA3 1HA

**Fife Enterprise**                    01592 621000
Kingdom House, Saltire Centre, Glenrothes, Fife KY6 2AQ

**Forth Valley Enterprise**                    01786 451919
Laurel House, Laurelhill Business Park, Stirling FK7 9JQ

**Glasgow Development Agency**                    0141 204 1111
Atrium Court, 50 Waterloo Street, Glasgow G2 6HQ

**Grampian Enterprise Ltd**                    01224 211500
27 Albyn Place, Aberdeen, AB1 1YL

**Lanarkshire Development Agency**                    01698 745454
New Lanarkshire House, Willow Drive, Strathclyde Business Park, Bellshill
ML4 3AD

**Lothian and Edinburgh Enterprise Ltd**                    0131 313 4000
Apex House, 99 Haymarket Terrace, Edinburgh EH12 5HD

**Renfrewshire Enterprise Company**                    0141 848 0101
25-29 Causeyside St, Paisley PA1 1UL

**Scottish Borders Enterprise**                    01896 758991
Bridge St, Galashiels TD1 1SW

**Scottish Enterprise Tayside**                    01382 223100
Enterprise House, 45 North Lindsay St, Dundee DD1 1HT

# APPENDIX C
# WEEKLY BENEFIT RATES 1997/98

## Income Support/Income-based JSA Personal Allowances
Single person aged 16 or 17
    lower rate . . . . . . . . . . . . . . . . . . . . . . . £29.60
    higher rate . . . . . . . . . . . . . . . . . . . . . . £38.90
Single person aged 18–24 . . . . . . . . . . . . . . . . £38.90
Single person aged 25 and over . . . . . . . . . . . . . £49.15

Lone parent aged 16 or 17
    lower rate . . . . . . . . . . . . . . . . . . . . . . . £29.60
    higher rate . . . . . . . . . . . . . . . . . . . . . . £38.90
Lone parent aged 18 or over . . . . . . . . . . . . . . £49.15
Couple both aged under 18 . . . . . . . . . . . . . . . £58.70
Couple one or both aged 18 or over . . . . . . . . . . £77.15

Dependent child
    until Sept following 11th birthday . . . . . . . . . . . £16.90
    from Sept following 11th birthday to Sept following
    16th birthday . . . . . . . . . . . . . . . . . . . . . £24.75
    from Sept following 16th birthday to day before
    19th birthday . . . . . . . . . . . . . . . . . . . . . £29.60

Dependent children with protected rates
    age 11 before 7th April 1997 . . . . . . . . . . . . . £24.75
    age 16 before 7th April 1997 . . . . . . . . . . . . . £29.60
    age 18 before 7th April 1997 . . . . . . . . . . . . . £38.90

## Premiums
Family premium . . . . . . . . . . . . . . . . . . . . . £10.80
Family premium (lone parent rate) . . . . . . . . . . . £15.75
Disability premium: single . . . . . . . . . . . . . . . £20.95
Disability, premium, couple . . . . . . . . . . . . . . . £29.90
Disabled child premium . . . . . . . . . . . . . . . . . £20.95

*continued* ...

## Premiums continued
Severe disability premium:
 single . . . . . . . . . . . . . . . . . . . . . . . . £37.15
 couple, one qualifies . . . . . . . . . . . . . . . . £37.15
 couple, both qualify . . . . . . . . . . . . . . . . . £74.30

## Statutory Sick Pay
Earnings threshold . . . . . . . . . . . . . . . . . . . £62.00
Standard rate . . . . . . . . . . . . . . . . . . . . . . £55.70

## Incapacity Benefit
Long-term . . . . . . . . . . . . . . . . . . . . . . . . £62.45
Short-term (under pension age)
 lower rate . . . . . . . . . . . . . . . . . . . . . . £47.10
 higher rate . . . . . . . . . . . . . . . . . . . . . . £55.70

## Invalidity Allowance (transitional)
High rate . . . . . . . . . . . . . . . . . . . . . . . . £13.15
Middle rate . . . . . . . . . . . . . . . . . . . . . . . . £8.30
Lower rate . . . . . . . . . . . . . . . . . . . . . . . . £4.15

## Severe Disablement Allowance
Severe Disablement Allowance . . . . . . . . . . . . . £37.15
Age related addition,
 high rate . . . . . . . . . . . . . . . . . . . . . . . £13.15
 middle rate . . . . . . . . . . . . . . . . . . . . . . £8.10
 lower rate . . . . . . . . . . . . . . . . . . . . . . . £4.05

## Invalid Care Allowance
Invalid Care allowance . . . . . . . . . . . . . . . . . £37.35
Increase for adult dependant . . . . . . . . . . . . . . £21.90

## Child Benefit
Eldest or only child: couple . . . . . . . . . . . . . . £11.05
Eldest or only child: lone parent . . . . . . . . . . . . £17.10
Each subsequent child . . . . . . . . . . . . . . . . . . £9.00

# REFERENCES

The abbreviations of the legislation used in this Guide are not officially recognised, so it is advisable to use the full title when writing letters. We do not include legislation which simply amends earlier legislation.

Readers who wish to look up the legislation can do so in the eleven-volume *The Law Relating to Social Security* (the 'Blue Volumes'), which is published by The Stationery Office (formerly HMSO) and kept up to date by regular supplements. Most large libraries have a copy. Your local Department of Social Security (DSS) office has a copy which you are allowed to look at.

Otherwise, you could consult either:

*Non-Means-Tested Benefits: The Legislation*, 1996 by D Bonner, I Hooker and R White (Sweet & Maxwell, 1996); or

*Income Related Benefits Legislation 1996, by J Mesher and D Wood (Sweet and Maxwell, 1996).*

(Updated editions will be published in October 1997.)

These set out the most useful legislation with detailed commentaries. They are available from the Child Poverty Action Group and each publication costs £53.50 including a supplement (1997 editions £42.50 if ordered before July) (1-5 Bath Street, London EC1V 9PY).

## Legislation and Regulations

**CB (Gen) Regs**: The Child Benefit (General) Regulations.

**Disability Act 95:** Disability Discrimination Act, 1995.

**Emp Act 89:** Employment Act, 1989.

**EP Act 78:** Employment Protection (Consolidation) Act 1978, as amended by the Employment Acts of 1980, 1982 and 1988.

**H&S Act 74:** Health and Safety at Work etc. Act, 1974.

**H&S Regs 90:** Health and Safety (Training for Employment) Regulations 1990

**IS (Gen) Regs**: The Income Support (General) Regulations 1987, as amended.

**IS (Gen) (JSA) Regs**: The Income Support (General) (Jobseeker's Allowance Consequential Amendments) Regulations 1996

**JSA Regs**: The Jobseeker's Allowance Regulations 1996.

**JS Act 95**: Jobseeker's Act, 1995

**RR Act 76**: Race Relations Act, 1976

**SD Act 75**: Sex Discrimination Act, 1975

**SS Act 88**: Social Security Act, 1988.

**SSC&B Act 92**: Social Security Contributions and Benefits Act 1992.

## Other publications

**AFA:** TEC Annual Funding Agreement, 1996, DfEE.

**AOG:** *Adjudication Officers' Guide*, 13 volumes published by the Stationery Office and updated by regular supplements.

**ES APG:** *Employment Service Allowance Payments Guide November 1996,* Employment Service.

**ESG 36:** *Training Programmes*, ES Guide 36, updated March 1994, Employment Service.

**ESG 39:** *Advising Clients*, ES Guide 39, Amendment 7, November 1995, Employment Service.

**Hansard/Hansard WA:** Hansard House of Commons Debates and Hansard Written Answers – published on a daily and weekly basis and available from the Stationery Office (formerly HMSO) bookshops or by post from PO Box 276, London SW8 5DT.

**JSA 16/17:** *JSA for 16 and 17 year olds, 1996.* Benefits Agency and Employment Service.

**TEC PP:** *TEC & CCTE Planning Prospectus: Requirements & Guidance 1997-98.* Revised 28 February 1997.

**TEC Standards:** *Draft TEC & CCTE Standards Guide*, Version 2, 4 December 1996.

**TEC QA:** *TEC Quality Assurance: Supplier Management, Requirements of the Employment Department*, Quality Assurance Division, TEED, Employment Department. 1993

**TEC STN:** *The TEC Special Training Needs Strategy, A Developing Good Practice Guide for TECs*, Employment Department.

# *Unemployment and Training Rights Handbook*

The *Guide to Training and Benefits for Young People* is published with a companion volume – the *Unemployment and Training Rights Handbook*.

Published by the Unemployment Unit, this volume is as detailed and referenced as the Guide and is aimed at people aged 18 and over. It focuses mainly on the procedures and programmes operated through the Department for Education and Employment, with comprehenisve information on Jobseeker's Allowance, which is available through ES Jobcentres. It also includes a good deal of information on Income Support, which is available through the Department of Social Security. It comprehensively explains:

◆ the rights and responsibilities of unemployed people including the effects of recent changes to benefits legislation, including JSA, and the Employment Service;

◆ the procedures to follow if you are not in full-time work and wish to claim benefit;

◆ the various training and employment schemes that are available to unemployed people aged 18 and over and the rights of the participants on schemes.

For prices and order form, see page 151.

# Working Brief

Keep up to date with changes to the employment and training schemes, legislation and benefit rules covered by this Guide.

*Working Brief* is the monthly journal of Youthaid and the Unemployment Unit. It reports on developments in employment, training, benefits and the labour market. Its circulation of over 2000 is drawn from training and welfare rights organisations, economic agencies, TECs, Westminster and Government.

*Working Brief* regularly scoops the other specialist journals to publish detailed analysis of:
◆ figures from YT and TfW leaver surveys;
◆ the state of the YT Guarantee;
◆ ethnic unemployment rates;
◆ TfW and YT funding;
◆ severe hardship and YT Bridging Allowance payments;
◆ outcomes from Restart interviews;
◆ equal opportunities in YT and TfW;
◆ disqualifications under Actively Seeking Work;
◆ Careers Service reviews;
◆ unemployment among people with disabilities;
◆ inner city job schemes;
◆ details of TEC and Government negotiations.

Every edition of *Working Brief* contains a labour market analysis. It gives quarterly results from the YT and TfW leaver surveys, Youthaid's estimates of young people without an income and the Labour Force Survey analyses. Annual features show the costs of unemployment, reviews of the Employment Service performance and analysis of the TEC contracts.

For subscription rates and order form, see page 151.

# *Order form*

If you want to place an order or ask for further information, please tear out or photocopy this page and the next.

Send them to **Youthaid, 322 St John Street, London EC1V 4NT.**

Name/Address: . . . . . . . . . . . . . . . . . . . . . . . . . . . . . .

. . . . . . . . . . . . . . . . . . . . . . . . . . . . . . . . . . . . .

. . . . . . . . . . . . . . . . . . . . Postcode: . . . . . . .

Please enclose payment, making cheques payable to Youthaid. Please allow 14 days for postal delivery. All prices include postage and packing.

One year's subscription to *Working Brief* (ISSN 09566120)

£45 statutory and commercial organisations

£35 voluntary and non-profit organisations

£25 individual at private address

*Guide to Training and Benefits for Young People* (£6.95)

*Unemployment and Training Rights Handbook* (£9.95)

The above Guide and Handbook ordered together (£15.95)

Enclosed £ . . . . . . . Cheque number: . . . . . . . . . . . .

Please Turn Over

# *Further information*

For details of other Unemployment Unit and Youthaid publications and services, please indicate below. Please make sure that you have filled in the address panel on the previous page. Return the form to the address given there.

☐ Information about revised editions of both the *Unemployment and Training Rights Handbook* and the *Guide to Training and Benefits for Young People*

☐ Further information about Youthaid and the Unemployment Unit and other publications

☐ Details of training courses – covering benefits, training schemes, labour market data, new Government policy, TECs/LECs – designed for guidance and advice agencies, policy makers and training providers.

To help us assess the most effective ways of getting information to readers, we would be grateful if you could indicate how you received a copy of this Guide:

☐ Direct mail order from Youthaid and the Unemployment Unit

☐ Bookshop purchase

☐ Leaflet inserted in a mailing from another organisation or magazine

☐ Centrally purchased in bulk by an organisation

☐ From a magazine advertisement